If You Don't Like Your Life,

Change It!

Kabbalah Publishing is a registered DBA of
The Kabbalah Centre International, Inc.

For further information:

The Kabbalah Centre
1062 S. Robertson Blvd., Los Angeles, CA 90035
155 E. 48th St., New York, NY 10017

1.800.Kabbalah www.kabbalah.com

First Trade Paper Edition, May 2013

Printed in Canada

ISBN: 978-1-57189-875-3
ebook ISBN: 978-1-57189-881-4

Design: HL Design (Hyun Min Lee) www.hldesignco.com

100%

If You Don't Like Your Life,
Change It!

Using Kabbalah to Rewrite the Movie of Your Life

My Life

KABBALAH
PUBLISHING

Yehuda Berg

Bestselling author of *The Power of Kabbalah*

Table of Contents

Introduction

Directing Your Own Movie

Life isn't something that just happens to you; it's a movie that you yourself are creating. That's also true for me, and for everyone else, too. But most of us settle for minor roles. We do this because of the self-limiting beliefs we formed during childhood when we didn't know any better. Now, as adults, it's time for us to take another look at the life we've created. If you don't like yours, now's your chance to put it through rewrite to make it more real, more fun, and more fulfilling. Change it!

Like a film, your life is shaped by the perspective you choose. This is why two siblings can experience the same childhood events but interpret them so differently. It's also the reason that we're so deeply affected by people like Mohandas (Mahatma) Gandhi, Helen Keller, and Christopher Reed, who all took the difficult and painful raw material of their lives and shaped it in ways that inspire the rest of us to do more with our own.

Greatness is what we achieve when we fight our way through difficulty, and since we've all done that at some time in our life, we've all got greatness inside us. You certainly do. And the measure of that greatness is the size of the challenges you overcome. To put it simply, the more messed up your life feels today, the more satisfying, rewarding, and joyful you can make it tomorrow.

You're not to blame for the problems in your life, but you are responsible for the movie that is your life. You can add scenes or cut them, or you can rewrite the script completely. You can fire or give a smaller role to that actor who requires too much coddling, or disrupts the shoot, or drains everyone's enthusiasm. This is your movie, your life. You're calling the shots. You can change everything from this moment on, regardless of what has happened in the past.

Yes, many of us have suffered through difficult and painful childhoods. As a teacher at The Kabbalah Centre, I've talked with hundreds of people and heard their tragic stories of abuse, violence, tragedy, and illness; these are far more common than you may realize. It's difficult to examine our childhood baggage to see how those early lessons we taught ourselves were distorted by what we needed to believe in order to feel safe or even to survive. But in the end, they were just make-believe stories we told ourselves to make sense of a world we were too young to understand.

The truth comes down to this: You are directing this movie of your life. You always have been because every scene has been filmed through your unique lens. It's yours and yours alone. Understanding this takes digging, accepting, and letting go—deep emotional and spiritual work. True, such work is often painful, but what could possibly be more important? The alternative is sleepwalking through this lifetime and missing out on its precious joys and opportunities.

Right now is the best possible time to start re-scripting your life, so let's begin the job of re-making your movie by posing a question: What do you appreciate about your life? Don't over-think the answer; just quickly jot down the first five things that come to mind. The key to adding things to this list—to growing the number of things you're happy about—is shifting how you perceive the difficult things in your life, the things you're *not* happy about. For example, if you have problems with a co-worker, instead of focusing on what this person is doing to you, ask yourself this: What lesson is this unpleasant colleague here to teach me? Perhaps I need to learn patience, or new communication skills, or how to stand up for myself.

Difficult situations are like flags indicating where your soul's work lies, and with a little shift in perspective, you can come to appreciate that they're here to help you grow into your full potential.

The Spiritual Path

Very few people turn to spirituality out of curiosity or a passing interest. Most of us start on a spiritual path because we have problems we haven't been able to resolve on our own: A failing marriage, an illness, a family tragedy, the loss of a job, struggles with our children. Unfortunately, once the problem resolves—the relationship ends or the sickness passes—our spiritual commitment tends to fizzle along with it. We're no longer motivated to do the difficult spiritual work.

When we turn to spirituality just to solve a particular problem, we won't succeed over the long term. But if we appreciate the process—how much the technology behind an ancient wisdom like Kabbalah can do for us every day of our lives, for example—we can stay motivated; nothing flashy, just steady progress, step by step. You'll be amazed by how much power you'll discover inside yourself.

Moses turned to God to create a spectacular miracle: As many as 3,000,000 Israelites walked through the middle of the Red Sea to escape the chariots of the mighty Egyptian army. Yet even after this, the greatest show on Earth, only two Israelites entered the land of Israel. Still, Moses kept his faith, and today we recognize him as one of the greatest souls ever to walk this Earth.

As you learn the basic system of Kabbalah and begin to put it to work, you'll soon see the difference it will start to make in your life. So try not to be in a hurry. If your interest is short-term, you're going to end up with little to show for your efforts. You'll end up like those Israelites in the desert who never made it to the land of milk and honey. But if your investment is long-term, you'll be amazed by how much power and Light you'll discover inside yourself.

If you've read any of my other books or heard me speak, you know that I'm a storyteller. I learn through stories myself, so it's natural for me to teach with them. I've sprinkled some of my favorite stories throughout this book, and I ask you to please read them closely, even if you've heard or read them before. Stories are an aspect of kabbalistic technology that helps us gauge the level of our consciousness and then elevate it. Each time we hear a story, we can learn something new from it based on where we are.

Before we go further, let me give you a quick primer on Kabbalah, my source for the insights in this book. Kabbalah's historical roots lie in secret mystical teachings that are thousands of years old, but what we teach and practice at The Kabbalah Centre today is far more accessible. Thanks to the efforts of Rav Brandwein, my father's teacher, and my father and mother, Rav and Karen Berg, Kabbalah is now available to anyone from any religious background who is interested in learning a spiritual system that not only adds meaning and context to their lives but also joins them in community with other like-minded people.

Here's a quick rundown of the basic principles of Kabbalah.

- First, and probably most importantly, Kabbalah differentiates between immediate gratification, which is superficial, and long-term fulfillment. This allows us to pursue a deeper, more enduring kind of happiness.

- Next, we learn to identify our ego and its workings, and how to apply some powerful tools to pry ourselves free from its grip. Ego drives our reactive behavior, which keeps us entangled in everyday chaos, ignorant of the deeper reasons for the events in our lives. Our ego, sometimes personified in Kabbalah as the Opponent, functions best when we feel victimized by experience, and it takes a back seat only when we take more responsibility for our own lives.

- It turns out that the world we live in—the physical reality we experience through our senses—represents only 1% of what's really going on. The other 99% is the spiritual dimension, where the Light, the spiritual source of all Creation, resides. This has tremendous implications that we'll explore in detail further on, but for now it's enough to know that an endless world of answers, inspiration, energy, truth, love, and well-being exists beyond the chaos, pain, and suffering of everyday life. And we can learn to tap into that spiritual realm whenever we need to.

- The Light is the source of everything. It brought the universe into being, but on a more practical level, the Light is the energy of our soul. It's the love we exchange with family and friends. It's the wellspring of our inspiration, creativity, and financial success; it's the joy and satisfaction we find in life.

- Our spiritual garbage—the stuff that blocks us from connecting to the Light—is actually a gift that points out what we need to correct in our own consciousness. This correction is the reason our souls came into this particular lifetime.

- We are all receivers. Our souls are essentially vessels for the energy of the Light. Kabbalah says that for all the many decisions we appear to make in life, we are really making only one fundamental choice: Do I want to receive this energy for myself alone or am I bringing this energy into my life to share with others? This decision determines how much Light we will receive.

- Finally, all of us are connected with each other—and to everything everywhere—through an invisible spiritual network. Every action, every vibration in this web of energy, has an effect. When we judge other people harshly or mistreat them, we bring pain and chaos not only into their lives but also into our own. On the other hand, when we share selflessly, we increase everyone's measure of Light, peace, and happiness.

This book is organized into three parts. The first is intended to help us break the bonds of habitual thinking that keep all of us stuck in place. The jailer has long since unlocked the door and abandoned the prison but here we sit in our cells, captives of the belief that freedom is no longer possible.

Once we've opened our cell doors, the second section shows what we're up against, and how overcoming obstacles releases new Light in our lives. Each chapter in this section reveals the unique benefits associated with a particular type of obstacle.

The third section is a spiritual toolbox in which we'll find the kabbalist's tricks of the trade—ways to benefit from knowing the system through which the Light does its work.

Freedom; knowledge of the obstacles that lie ahead and their hidden benefits are a toolkit to ease our way. It is my greatest hope that the three sections of this book will provide what you need to realize that perception is the key—in movies and in life—and that by seeing the truth of things more deeply, you can rewrite your own script to fulfill the deepest desires of your heart and soul.

Part One

Assuming the Director's Chair

Chapter 1

Breaking Free

Now that you've chosen to direct a new movie of your life, let's start by examining the specific steps necessary to make this happen in order to lead to a real transformation in consciousness. The first is to become aware that we're all born into this world with preprogrammed modes of behavior. Mostly we're hardwired for short-term, immediate gratification, which has obvious benefits in terms of survival: Safety and a full belly come first. But once those requirements have been met, this kind of wiring can be counter-productive when it comes to satisfying our higher needs for connection, meaning, and purpose. So let's take a closer look at how we're programmed and at what we can do to change that hardwiring wherever it impedes our progress. Replacing our long-established behaviors won't be easy. We're going to need to expose our old conditioning, jackhammer it up, and replace it with patterns that support the life we want. Repetition is the best way to reinforce a new neuronal pathway in the brain, so it will be particularly helpful in supporting the new, more accurate beliefs that we'll be putting in place to supplant the old.

Expanding Our Vessel

When we're born into this world, we're full of endless potential. But as we're being socialized during childhood, we learn to limit ourselves, which from a kabbalistic perspective means that we no longer open our vessel to all the Light that the universe intends for us.

This reminds me of elephants in a circus. When they're not working, their trainers keep them from wandering by tethering them to a small peg in the ground. It's ludicrous, though, to see these massive elephants restrained by these tiny wooden pegs when the slightest tug would send that peg flying out of the ground. Why doesn't that happen?

The secret is how the elephant was raised. When the elephant was a baby, the trainer used the very same peg, but at that age, the baby elephant couldn't pull it out of the ground. This idea was reinforced daily by the trainer, so that today, when it would be easy for the elephant to tear free of the peg, that possibility doesn't even cross its mind.

All too many of us conduct our lives the same way. Tethered in childhood, we've convinced ourselves that we can't break free and live the full life we really want. But kabbalists say there are no limits to what we can do when we're freed from our self-limiting views.

We can see this clearly when it comes to money. Money is one of the most misunderstood objects of all, which makes it one of the greatest sources of stress, negativity, and victim-consciousness. It doesn't have to be this way, though. The most important thing to know about money is that it's a form of energy, and our job is to create a large enough vessel to draw down an abundance of that energy. This sounds pretty abstract, I know, so let's take a closer look at how this works.

Like everything else in this world, money follows the rule of 1% and 99%: It's made up of 1% matter and 99% energy. How many people do you know in your life that have plenty of money and still aren't happy? They've got the 1%, the material part, but they don't know how to derive its blessings. They could have billions and still wouldn't be any happier. It's important for us, then, to learn how to receive the potential energy that resides in material things like money. If we believe that money is the be-all and end-all rather than a gift from the Creator, then all money does is open the door to negativity. How many people are corrupted by money? It's one of the Opponent's favorite forms of bait—and most people go for it.

Since money, like everything else, must follow the 1%/99% rule, its primary power lies in the realm of the Light of the Creator. At this point you may be thinking, *That's all well and good, but how can I have more financial abundance in my life?* Try turning this question around a little: *If I don't have enough of the energy called money in my life, why not?*

Now think for a moment of all the reasons you might give for not having money in your life. Is it the way you were raised? The career you chose? Your boss? Is it financial trouble you got into that's now diverting money away from your real goals?

The problem with these questions is that they're all directed at the 1% aspect of money. If you understand that the power of money comes from the Light, you also know that the Light is infinite. It's endless. But for some reason, that endless abundance isn't making itself felt when it comes time to pay your bills.

Blocking the Light

So let's go back to the question: What's holding us back? What's keeping our vessel from connecting with the limitless abundance in the universe? The answer is *us*. We get in our own way. We block the Light. We keep the energy of money from making its way to us because our pipeline is choked with spiritual junk. When we clear away that garbage, however, we make room for prosperity, and the amount of Light we let in is directly related to the amount of garbage we remove.

We humans are creatures of habit, which means we can either develop conscious ways to encourage Light to come into our lives or fall into habits that invite in our Opponent (the ego) instead. By replacing unconscious routines that haven't been working for us with a more ordered way of being, we align ourselves with the 99% Realm of the spirit.

When we are born, our desires are simple. We want to eat, drink, and be comfortable (that wet diaper has got to be changed!). Everything is me, me, me. Oh, and by the way, I want it *now*. Over time, our needs get more complex, and we develop more sophisticated strategies for meeting those needs. But now we can take a closer look at those strategies and see how our desire to be comfortable (and to avoid discomfort) has been allowing the ego to dominate our decisions. Moreover, we can do something about this situation because by choosing to move the ego from the driver's seat into the passenger's seat, we step into the dimension of the 99%.

Challenge the Senses and Make Room for the Light

When I first began to study Kabbalah, I learned that when we're exploring our inner terrain, we can't rely on our five senses. We can't rely on our emotions. We can't rely on logic. I asked myself, *So what's left?* What's left, it turns out, is spirit. What's left is the soul's deep desire to connect and to grow. This higher level of consciousness is uncharted territory, but if we are courageous and have a strong enough desire to change our movie, we can access the 99% Realm of the spirit. The ego seeks to keep us on autopilot, but knowing there is an alternative, we can look for opportunities to move ourselves beyond the limited world of our physical senses and open ourselves up to channels of Light.

For example, you might have a situation at home where you believe your spouse is doing something wrong; in fact, everything you hear, see, and feel is telling you that this is not okay. You feel the impulse to respond the way you always do: With anger or judgment or frustration, or by simply shutting down. However, your deeper soul's desire and purpose is to become a more patient, tolerant person, so by getting in touch with that goal, you respond differently; perhaps you model the behavior you'd like to see in your spouse. This new and different response will result in a different experience for everyone involved. Try it and see what happens. Now that your soul's need is moving to center stage, the Light will come in to help you.

Small Steps

Even though research shows that deprivation diets don't work, people still talk nonstop about the latest weight-loss fad. Why don't diets work? Because they're short-term. They're not connected to a deeper purpose, unless, for example, being overweight has become a threat to your health. Sure, you may diet and lose some weight, but before long you've gained it back, along with a few extra pounds to boot. This is why it's more effective to connect with the reason your goal is meaningful to you—its spiritual purpose—and then embark on a series of small actions, baby steps that will change your life.

Albert Einstein is alleged to have responded to the question, "What do you consider to be man's greatest invention?" by saying, "Compound interest." Like compound interest, the benefits of the work of transformation emerge over time. We live in a society that bombards us with the message that we've got to have it—whatever *it* is—right now. And that if we buy this or enroll in that, we're going to see amazing results right away. But that's just Madison Avenue spin; it's not how things really work.

The student of a prominent kabbalist once said to him, "I'm doing everything humanly possible in my spiritual studies, but I still don't seem to be making any progress." The kabbalist responded by saying, "You're revealing more Light during the few hours you sleep than you are during your long day of study. Why? Because you're working so hard that you haven't left room for awareness. Sleep more, and when you're awake, consider what you're doing and why you are doing it. Then you'll see the Light at work in your life."

It's not what we do, but the consciousness with which we do it that makes the difference.

Shawshank

One of my favorite movies is *The Shawshank Redemption*. When wrongfully convicted, banker Andy Dufresne (played by Tim Robbins) decides to break out of prison. He takes a small rock hammer and starts chipping away at his cell wall. Keeping the hole covered by a poster of Rita Hayworth, Dufresne plans every aspect of his escape down to the last detail with patience and consistency.

I love this movie for many reasons. The story and acting are first-rate, but it's the themes that keep resonating in my mind: Being wrongfully imprisoned by the past, but refusing to be victimized by the situation; choosing to tirelessly pursue freedom; and ultimately finding fulfillment in the end. We're all walled in by our personal histories, but if rather than succumbing to a victim mentality we keep chipping away at those limitations, eventually we'll find a way through them. And life on the other side will be all the richer for the effort required to get there.

We can either go along to get along or we can rewrite the script. It's a choice each of us must make. The default position, unfortunately, is to keep sleepwalking through life.

Rewriting Your Script

Consider this question: If you died today, what legacy would you leave behind? What would you be remembered for? Take pen and paper and write your thoughts as quickly as you can, without stopping or editing yourself. Just scribble down whatever comes to mind.

Some of you may find this exercise difficult, either because you haven't given your legacy much thought or because you haven't been making decisions with it in mind. In either case, the very act of trying this exercise may provide you with valuable insights. Or perhaps the following questions will stimulate some ideas.

If you left this life today, how many real friends would you be leaving behind? How many people's lives would you have touched in a meaningful way? Did you do what you came into this world to do?

Think about it. Take your time. I'm looking for something more than just the specific items you'll be leaving behind.

Legacy is one good reason for directing your movie; it gives you a purpose. Become familiar with this purpose. Write it down. If you're feeling uncomfortable with its brevity, don't worry; as we continue, I'm sure you'll add to it. This particular exercise can help you make decisions on the journey that lies ahead. It can also uncover your deeper motivation for moving forward.

* * *

If you'd like to do some additional work on the garbage that keeps you from bringing more Light into your life, turn to the Appendix and do the first of the three exercises you'll find there.

Chapter 2

Taking Responsibility

Once you've started to see that freedom is possible, the next step is to assume full responsibility for what you do with it. We can't make significant script changes until we accept our authorship of every aspect of our movie. This isn't always easy to recognize, but it's essential.

One of the foundational principles of Kabbalah is that you don't have to go through life as a victim. Why do so many of us play the victim then? Because the role of victim provides certain benefits. (There's always a reason for what we do, even if this reason turns out not to be very good.) When you play the victim, you give yourself an out; you can't be blamed when something goes wrong. It's as if you're saying to the world, *How could I be responsible for what happened here? Can't you see that I'm an innocent bystander?*

However, by stepping out of the victim role, you gain a far larger benefit: You begin to make choices based on the deeper truth that you are the only one responsible for your happiness. You take the outcome into your own two hands.

Kabbalistically speaking, when we take on the role of cause, rather than that of effect, we are able to connect to the Cause of all Causes: the Light of the Creator, the Source of all that's good and joyful. When we're connected to this Source, we begin to regularly experience the magic of life.

Taking Responsibility, Assuming Control

Take a sheet of paper and a pencil, and list the things in your life that you know for sure are not your doing. Now ask yourself this: If you're not responsible for them, who is? Your parents? (Parents, by the way, will be the topic of the next chapter.) Could it be *possible* that you might have been responsible somehow, through your actions in this lifetime or in lifetimes past?

As we'll see, the answer is an emphatic yes. Kabbalah takes the position that you are 100% responsible for every experience in this lifetime. You create everything in your reality, and I mean *everything*. You create your dynamics at work, your dynamics in your love relationships, your dynamics with your family and friends. You're responsible for every aspect of your life—for better and for worse— even if it's a problem you were born with or something that happened to you when you were an infant or a child.

At this point, we're not going to get into *why* you're responsible. For now, it's enough to know that when something is part of our experience, we must take responsibility for it. This doesn't mean it's our fault. If someone abuses me, for instance, there's no reason to think I provoked it or encouraged it. But I do need to understand that once the experience has happened, how I perceive it is up to me. I can choose to blame myself for it—and become the victim. Or I can choose to believe that it's part of my movie for a reason—so that I can learn specific lessons from it. If I want to grow from it, I have to begin by taking responsibility.

In other words, we can choose to believe that the universe is random and chaotic. That's a personal decision each of us has to make. If, for you, life is a never-ending roll of the dice, I can't change that. But if you sometimes get the feeling that life isn't random, that things happen for a reason, I encourage you to stay with that thought. Fight the desire to make excuses. Connect to that deeper wisdom and hang on to it.

Perhaps at this point, you are thinking, *What is this guy talking about? How can I possibly be responsible for all the bad things that have happened to me? For my abusive parents, for my illnesses, for my tendencies toward anxiety or depression? Why would I choose any of that?*

Let me be clear about this: *You* are not to blame for the trauma in your life. However, I suggest that this trauma happened to you for a reason. The famous astrophysicist Stephen Hawking, who has had ALS for more than 40 years, says that if he hadn't been trapped in his dysfunctional body, he would never have had time to come up with his game-changing theories of the universe. It's up to you to figure out the lessons hidden in your experiences and to integrate these lessons into your life. This is how you begin to take responsibility. Then, once you've gone through this process of taking ownership, you can let those traumatic feelings go, once and for all.

If this is difficult to accept, I totally understand. But please stay with me on this. It will make more sense as we explore this idea in greater depth. The important thing right now is to become aware that you're not just a spectator. You're the driver. You're not just a face in a busy crowd scene, you're the director of this movie and you also play the lead role. It's your life. Owning it will give you a new degree of power, clarity, and joy.

Spiritual Lag Time

Why is it so difficult to see that we create everything that happens to us? Why do so many of us struggle with this spiritual principle? Why can't we accept the truth more easily?

The primary reason is a phenomenon known to kabbalists as *spiritual delay*, a concept that leads us to believe that our actions don't really have meaningful consequences. What is spiritual delay? We all know that time is not just the passage of minutes, hours, and days. We've all experienced firsthand that time can accelerate when we're having fun and drag interminably when we're struggling. In his book *A Brief History of Time*, astrophysicist Stephen Hawking alludes to this mysterious quality when he first mentions the word "time" by adding "whatever that is."

So what is time? Kabbalah defines time as the interval between cause and effect, between an event and its repercussions. Time can't exist without space, which is why in the spiritual realm, the 99%, where there is no matter or space, there is also no time, no beginning or end. But here in our physical dimension of the five senses, the 1% Realm, time plays a big role. Spiritually, this can work against us.

Let's imagine you've done something you regret. You may have been unkind or selfish, angry or greedy. After this unfortunate event, there's a delay caused by time, which ends when the effect of your harmful act makes itself felt. During this interval, however, you can lose track of the connection between your negative action and its result; then, when you, in turn, are the recipient of an act of selfish behavior, you may not realize that it originated with you.

But whether they manifest quickly or slowly, your actions do have consequences that will inevitably come back at you. In Eastern philosophy, this is known as karma, and it always comes back around.

Time: The Double-Edged Sword

There is also a beneficial aspect to the delay created by time. On the positive side, what does time give us? It gives us the ability to consider what happened. *Hey, I did something wrong here. I need to make amends for it, and I need to change the consciousness that led to that regrettable act.* This delay can advance the spiritual work, which is the reason why your soul came into this lifetime. If we lived in the 99% Realm where cause and effect are simultaneous, we wouldn't have this opportunity to learn from our mistakes.

A man who worked for NASA attended one of my classes at The Kabbalah Centre. He was a rocket scientist. Really. And when he heard this concept—the idea that time is the gap between cause and effect that gives us the opportunity for transformation—he said, "This one sentence has made this whole course worthwhile."

As we've seen, however, the interval between cause and effect can also work against us. If unused, it becomes a vacuum, and as we know, nature abhors a vacuum. In other words, when we create empty space without making an effort to fill it with Light, we're inviting a visit from the Opponent, our ego. Time can lead us to believe we're getting away with bad behavior. When we take advantage of a friend's generosity, tell a lie, or spread malicious gossip, and nothing bad happens, we're more likely to do it again. Time has covered up the truth that the repercussions of our bad deed are coming; they just haven't reached us yet.

If we looked at everything negative that we've done or embraced in this lifetime—all the jealousy, hatred, judgment, anger, and reactivity— and put them together, we'd be looking at a massive amount of toxic stuff. Everyone would because none of us is perfect and all of us have the potential to behave badly. When we take into consideration the negativity we've accumulated over many lifetimes, it's amazing that we still keep coming into the world as human beings capable of accomplishing great things. But thanks to the Creator, the gift of time gives us an opportunity to correct what we've done wrong.

Do We Create Illness?

When I mentioned earlier that taking ownership of your own movie includes assuming responsibility for illness (even chronic illness), you might have been asking yourself, *How could I create illness in my life, and why would I want to?* Or you may have been thinking, *Are you saying there's something wrong with me?*

The answer is no. But I am saying that you probably have insufficient knowledge about how life operates. That's why I'm offering you the insights of Kabbalah. You need to know more about cause and effect, about spiritual responsibility, and about connecting to lasting fulfillment. We've already seen that what we don't know can hurt us: When we don't see things clearly from a spiritual perspective, we make ourselves vulnerable to the chaos that's out there. So it's not that there's anything wrong with you; rather, it's lack of information that's keeping you from enjoying the fulfillment that exists right alongside you in the parallel spiritual world known as the 99%.

When we read some of the mind/body literature that's out there, we may find it increasingly difficult to deny the strong link between our mental state and our physical well-being. A famous long-term study was conducted on 1,800 healthy middle-aged men who worked at the Western Electric Plant in Chicago. In 1957, these workers took a personality test administered by psychologists, and over the following two decades, their health and lifestyles were carefully monitored. Researchers found that workers who initially scored high on the hostility scale were almost twice as likely to have a heart attack than workers with lower scores.

Those workers didn't have that information at the time, but we know it now. This gives us a chance to work on our feelings of hostility, to defuse them so we can improve our chances at a healthy heart. More importantly, we can see how illness serves as a messenger, telling us something we need to listen to. When my students are suffering from a common cold, I'll often ask them to consider why the cold bug may have hit them. So when you get a cold, ask yourself the following questions: What kinds of thoughts and feelings made your body a receptive home for this discomfort? What kind of consciousness? And what kind of shift is the cold asking you to make?

A Story of Soul Mates

Long ago in a small town in Russia, a wealthy man had a daughter so beautiful that young men couldn't tear their eyes away from her. When it came time for her to marry, she had countless suitors, but she wasn't taken with any of them. Then one day, a highly respected scholar came to visit. He was well liked by everyone, but he was an unlikely candidate for the young woman's hand; he was middle-aged and had a large wine-colored birthmark that covered much of his face. Opening the door to the scholar, the girl's father said, "Please, sir, I don't mean to be rude, but my daughter has already been visited by many young, handsome men from good families. With all due respect, I fear that you are wasting your time."

The scholar smiled kindly in response, his eyes twinkling. Then he said, "Thank you for your honesty. You're a good man. I ask only to speak with your daughter alone for five minutes, after which time I will gladly accept her decision."

Out of respect for the scholar, the father permitted him five minutes alone with his daughter. As the last moments ticked away, the doors to the drawing room were flung open and the radiant young woman rushed over to her father, hugging him as tears of joy streamed down her face. "Papa, we can begin preparing for a marriage feast. I have found the man with whom I will spend the rest of my life."

The father was stunned. As his daughter ran off to find her mother, he asked the scholar, "What did you say to her?"

"I told her the truth, that we are soul mates. I explained that when your daughter's soul and mine were preparing to enter this life, I saw she was destined to have a wine colored birthmark on her face. I knew her soul would struggle with that, so I took the mark on myself. When I told this to your daughter, her soul knew it to be true, and she recognized me for who I am and what I mean to her."

Inside each of us are things that may look like deformities—emotional, spiritual, and physical. Once we take responsibility for them, we've taken the first step to lasting change. Now the people around us will see us for who we really are, and not for those aspects of ourselves that we try to cover up.

This story teaches us that when things happen in this world that don't make sense, it's only because they're part of a universal system that extends far beyond anything we can see. When something happens to us, we may think, *There must be some mistake; that can't be my fate.* But there are no mistakes. Our job is to accept what happens, to take responsibility for it, and to learn the lesson it has come to teach us.

Rewriting Your Script

In this next exercise, I'd like to ask you to write down your answers to the following questions: What specific parts of your life are the least fulfilling? How might you be benefitting from this lack of fulfillment? In other words, if you had to look at the good side of these issues, what would you see? If you tend to get sick a lot, is it because it gets you more attention, buys you time away from work or frees you from certain responsibilities? What's in it for you?

Now just to warn you, when we ask these tough questions of ourselves and seek out the hidden truth, we may see aspects of ourselves we don't like. It's not fun to push past our own defenses, our ways of avoiding what we find unpleasant or painful. But we've got to do it. When we get to the bottom of the kinds of behavior that hold us back, we throw open the gates of change. Now we can rewrite our interpretation of events, removing the toxic effects of helplessness, anger, and blame from our lives.

For this chapter's script rewrite, make a note of the negative thoughts, actions, and feelings that were part of your life during the past month. Use your calendar to remind yourself of what took place. Don't edit your words and don't hold back. Just write down your thoughts as quickly as you can. If you need 15 pages to get it all down, that's fine.

When you finish writing, ask yourself what message these challenging moments might contain for you. Remember, your garbage—the collection of issues you came into this life to resolve—points out exactly where your opportunity lies to elevate your consciousness and connect to the Light.

Chapter 3

You Choose Your Parents (Really)

One of our most challenging tasks is taking responsibility for our relationship with our parents. It's so tempting to blame them instead. Parents make big targets. When we were little, they seemed colossal, all-powerful beings that strode through our lives, dispensing love and punishing transgressions. Then during our teenage years, they somehow went from godlike to foolish, and we had to oppose their suggestions at every turn.

Both of these distorted views of our parents contribute to the mistaken idea that our parents are somehow responsible for who and what we are.

At this point, the question I'd like to put to you is this: What do you blame your parents for? Don't give an off-the-cuff reaction. Think about it. Don't get too "spiritual" either. Be honest. Is there anything in your life that you blame on your parents? Is there anything you *don't* blame them for?

Kabbalistically, our parents are part of a system in which our souls reincarnate through many lifetimes. We came into this world specifically to learn spiritual lessons, some of them from our parents. In this sense, they are an exact match for us. When we push their buttons and they push ours, we're both participating in a process that is perfectly designed for spiritual growth on both sides.

Our soul knew this was a perfect match before it chose to inhabit our body. It's like those games you play as a toddler, where the wooden shapes fit only in the corresponding cutout spaces. Just as each of us has a unique set of fingerprints, so, too, is there just one parental match for every soul.

You might be thinking to yourself, *There's no way I would have ever chosen my parents.* But your soul, which made this choice on your behalf, operates on a different level from your everyday consciousness. It knows what you need to learn in this lifetime, and it chose the perfect environment for that correction to take place.

Unlike most people I know, I was born to parents who were already well along in their own spiritual journeys. My father Rav Berg is a prominent kabbalist, as is my mother. They set my brother and me on a spiritual path at an early age, which has been a tremendous blessing. But don't get me wrong. I, too, have my issues with my parents.

We all do. The first step is to discover what they are. In my case, my father and my mother were demanding. Of course, they have their baggage, too, and like the rest of us, they're doing the best they can with those issues. Some parents are skillful, and others less so; either way, they're going to push our buttons. But paying close attention to where our emotional buttons are located tells us exactly what we need to work on.

As children, we're closer to our original source in the Light, so we see our parents more lovingly. As we grow up, however, we tend to evaluate them more harshly. My father always liked to say that when we leave childhood behind, we become *adulterated*. We lose that innocence and openness that we had as kids. We become judgmental.

This is not to say that a good relationship with parents is extraordinary. But even if you're already enjoying a close relationship with your parents, the spiritual work you're doing can make it better, bringing even more Light into your life.

Thinking about Your Parents

Okay. Now let's get to work. Find a quiet place where you won't be disturbed and turn off your cell phone. Take a few deep breaths to clear your mind. Now take some time to think about the things that you don't like about your parents: Their failings, the things they do that annoy you, upset you or leave you cold.

After giving this full consideration, now consider the things you love about your parents. Bring those qualities to the forefront of your mind without filters, without qualification. The mere fact that your parents brought you into this world makes them worthy of appreciation. Every person has good in them. See the good in your parents.

Ask yourself this: Where and how do I relate to people in the same way that I relate to my parents? If issues you have with your parents are also showing up in your other relationships, make a note of them now.

Now ask yourself how and where your parents relate to other people in the same way they relate to you. I know it's not easy to see your parents' behavior with any degree of perspective, but set aside your tendency to judge them and try to consider them with simple curiosity. This isn't just about you. Whatever issues your parents may have, they may have with everyone; those ways of being in the world may be heightened by the intensity of the parent-child relationship, but they will also be reflected in your parents' friendships, their work lives, and their relationships with other family members.

It's important to map out where your parents consistently come into conflict with you, and where and how those same issues show up in their dealings with other people. Even though it may seem as if they're much nicer to everyone else, you'll find after a little digging that the qualities you see in your parents also inform their other relationships.

The Difficulties of Parenting and Being Parented

I'm sure you've noticed that people who are overly controlling, or who act tough, or who are angry or hostile much of the time aren't really coming from a place of inner strength. Invariably, they're overcompensating for a sense of their own weakness, a feeling that if they don't protect themselves, they'll be overwhelmed. This is true for parents, too. It's their own weaknesses as people that lead them to become controlling, frustrated, angry, and disconnected. It's really not about us at all. Their struggle with us is just part of their struggle to find the strength to deal with the difficulties they face. Parenting isn't easy, and it tends to bring unresolved baggage to the surface, as you know if you're already a parent yourself.

So what's the solution? We need to make space between ourselves and our parents in order to see them as people in their own right, beyond the roles they play in our lives. We have our own path and so do they, and much of what affects us is just our parents being on their path. For example, if they tend to feel easily threatened, they may feel it most keenly with us because we've already slipped under many of their defenses. We're already inside the castle walls.

This explains how our parents can be so nice to total strangers, to that waiter in the restaurant or that cashier at the grocery store, while you're asking yourself, *Why can't they treat me that way?* But when we look a little more closely, we see that same phenomenon at work in ourselves. Often, we behave a lot better with acquaintances—or with people we don't even know—than we do with our closest friends, our siblings, our parents or our mates.

We can gain some insight into why this is the case, but the bottom line is that this behavior is upside down. It's essential that we be our best selves with the people who are closest to us. Family is family, no matter what. Best friends are best friends. These are the people we need to work with and be with to become fulfilled and happy and successful—and we need to help them do the same. Somehow, however, the Opponent has tricked us into this perverse dynamic where we treat a complete stranger or an acquaintance better than we do our closest friend or family member.

One way parents create problems for us is by living vicariously through us, their children. Mom may have had the potential to be a great violin player, but for some reason, that dream never came to pass. So now her child has to start at age three with Suzuki violin lessons, like it or not. Mom couldn't do it, so her child is burdened with the task. In cases like this, we are trying to direct our own *tikkun*, our soul's correction, at our children. Because we didn't live fully ourselves, we want our children to live for us.

Of course, this is terribly unfair. We can chart whatever course we want for ourselves, but our job as parents is to encourage our children to be themselves, to live their lives, not ours. When we lose sight of this, we put tremendous pressure on our kids, doing them a great disservice.

When we look at our own parents we can use this insight to take some pressure off ourselves. We are not responsible for their behavior. My dad may have forced me to play baseball because he loved it as a kid, but that doesn't make me a victim. And I learned a lot from it: Discipline, the pleasures of exercise, and insight into my father, to name just a few things. With the right spiritual consciousness, you can take whatever your parents gave you by way of a childhood, find the good in it, and apply that to what you want to do with your life, to the path you choose in order to share your Light with the world.

Bad as it may be, sometimes having an abusive parent isn't as difficult as trying to understand the other parent, the one who stood passively by and watched the abuse take place or turned a blind eye to it. How could a parent in that situation do nothing? It's easy to see how children from abusive families can lose faith in people and come to see the world as an unpredictable and dangerous place.

But once again, difficult though this may be to appreciate, it's not about you. So we have to keep asking ourselves, *Why is this part of my movie? Why is it happening to me? Why did my soul choose this family, this environment, to grow up in? What spiritual good can I find in it?*

As we know, from a kabbalistic perspective, the more difficult the situation, the greater the potential for immense Light to be revealed. When you look at your life this way, you'll see that whatever's there has been presented to you as an opportunity. Nothing has been given to you that you can't handle. No matter what your parents went through, no matter what you went through with your parents, it happened for a reason. Our job in this lifetime is not to fix our parents; it's to make peace with them or what they've done, so they no longer push our buttons, and then to discover what we need to learn from them. When we change our perspective, our camera angle, so that we can see the times we felt hurt and victimized as actual blessings, we literally transform those seeds of experiences that were planted in our past. And as we change the seed, the tree will also change.

By going back to those negative experiences and injecting them with Light, by seeing the good in them, by taking responsibility for them and growing accordingly, we can actually change the DNA of the seeds sown during our childhood. This works because it is our perspective, our consciousness, which determines our reality. What matters is not what happened, but what we think and feel about what happened, and fortunately, that is what we can transform.

Rewriting Your Script

Let's do some rewriting around this. Breathe deeply, relax, and ask yourself why your soul chose these particular parents for you. What lessons have you learned from the way they raised you or didn't raise you? What lessons could you still learn today? Think about it. Be open to the answers and let them come to you from that larger place where the spirit resides, where you're not restricted by the filters of ego. Be curious.

This isn't an easy process, not for anyone. It's not easy for me, and my parents were enlightened people with lots of spiritual tools at their disposal. Sometimes I can see why I chose them, but I have more difficulty understanding why they chose me. Why would such spiritual people bring my soul into their lives? When I find myself getting stuck on that thought, I realize that I'm taking on too much. Solving that mystery is not what I'm here to do. My job is to figure out what work *my* soul came here to do—my kabbalistic *tikkun*, or correction—and then to strive to complete it.

When you focus on the reasons why you chose your parents, you shift power from them to you. You become the cause, not merely the effect. It's time to make that shift in the dynamic for your own well-being. Who knows, maybe your changes will inspire your parents to become the cause in their own lives. And when they do, you'll be able to enjoy a truly awesome relationship together.

In the process of sifting through these issues, things may get worse for you before they get better. This's quite typical. You're stirring up powerful feelings you pushed aside long ago, when you weren't capable of understanding what was really going on. Now you are. The good news is that the tumult will settle down, and things will get better. Much better. Life is so much richer when we embrace it as active agents rather than victims.

Write down what you've turned up with your inquiry. Why *did* you choose your parents? What new actions can you take now that you have this knowledge? Whatever actions you do take, you'll see things start to shift in your life to reflect the changes you're bringing to your experience.

* * *

If you'd like to do some more work around parents, turn to the Appendix and try the second of the three exercises you'll find there.

Part Two
Negotiating the Obstacles

Chapter 4

The Difficulty of Revealing Light

The Story of the Briefcase and the Light

The following story is one of my favorite ways to illustrate how our actions do or don't reveal Light. It describes three scenarios, each showing a different decision being made in a particular situation. As you're reading, consider which decision would reveal more Light for the individual involved and for the world.

Let's set the stage. Imagine a corporate office at the end of the day. Everybody's eager to go home, so there's a lot of activity and confusion. The receptionist has already left, but someone has left a brown leather briefcase on her desk.

Scenario #1. A man walks by and notices the briefcase. He walks over and unlatches it, only to discover that it's crammed with bundles of hundred-dollar bills. He quickly looks around to confirm that no one has noticed him, picks up the briefcase, and walks away.

Scenario #2. Same setting, end of the day. A man walks by, sees the briefcase sitting on the reception desk, opens it up, and finds that it's filled with hundred-dollar bills. His hands are trembling as he snaps the latches shut. No one pays any attention as he takes the briefcase, but he's clearly uncomfortable with his decision. A few moments later, he returns to the reception desk, puts the briefcase back where he found it, and walks away.

Scenario #3. A man walks by reception at the end of the day. He sees a briefcase on the desk and opens it up to look for any signs of identification. Nothing but bundles of cash. He closes the case and takes it, replacing it with a note: *I found your briefcase and have removed it for safe-keeping. If you can tell me precisely what is in it, I will be happy to return it to you.* He adds his phone extension, locks the case in his office, and goes home.

Again, the question is this: In which scenario was the most Light revealed? Many people hearing this story for the first time say that the third person revealed the largest amount of Light. He handled the situation with integrity and competence. He did his best to ensure the return of the briefcase to its legitimate owner.

But the question we're asking here is not who is the most spiritual person; the question is: In which scenario was the most spiritual energy revealed?

Let's review what we now know. We know that the greater the transformation, the larger the amount of Light revealed. So in which scenario do we see the biggest change taking place? In scenario #1, the man started off with no scruples and ended up the same way. No transformation there. He's a thief from start to finish. In scenario #2, the man gave in to his desire to take the money, but he was conflicted about it and changed his mind. In scenario #3, a principled man acted in a principled way.

So where's the transformation? It's in scenario #2.

This story illustrates the surprising kabbalistic point that virtue itself doesn't generate the most Light. The size of the transformation or the degree of difficulty to be surmounted, determines how much Light is revealed. The situation with the briefcase posed no problem for the first or third man, but the second one had to dig deep to overcome his first impulse to take the money. He wrestled with his first reaction and overcame it. He faced a big obstacle and fought his way through it.

This is what reveals Light, and this is the special opportunity provided by the obstacles you'll be learning about in the upcoming chapters in Part Two.

Everyone's Situation Is Unique

A lot of people who begin doing spiritual work find themselves struggling to continue. Often, this is because they feel they're seeing only modest results despite all the effort they're putting in. But there is no one-size-fits-all when it comes to transformation. And transformation is often not dramatic. As I mentioned before, progress takes place in lots of little ways and baby steps.

For every person, those actions are going to be different. When a homeless person gives five dollars to someone who's even worse off, this generates far more Light than the billionaire who gives away $1,000,000. The spiritual energy released by our actions depends on how difficult it is for us individually. If I have an addiction to alcohol and I take steps to fight it, doing so will bring me far more fulfillment than it would for someone who stops drinking but didn't much like it anyway.

This is one of the differences between religion and spirituality. Religion makes rules that are meant to apply to everyone. By contrast, a spiritual framework like the one provided by Kabbalah offers general insights into how the world works, but we, as individuals, must find our own way to apply them.

Bread of Shame

When you first hear the phrase "Bread of Shame," it sounds as if this core kabbalistic concept may have something to do with baked goods. But Bread of Shame is really a feeling—that uncomfortable sense of shame or discomfort that comes from receiving something you haven't earned. You just got promoted because your boss likes you, not because you're doing great work. You scored high on that test because you cheated, not because of your command of the material. Someone gave you a lot of money for no particular reason. Bread of Shame is a universal law. It states that whatever we receive without earning will never fulfill us in the long term. Bread of Shame is one of the reasons that lottery winners, for example, have so much difficulty finding happiness after hitting the big jackpot.

When you get something for nothing, a couple of things happen:

1. You won't appreciate it because you didn't put anything into it, and

2. It's harder for you to attract and retain more Light.

Imagine that you're a professional golfer. One day, you find an old golf club in a pawnshop and buy it. When you take it to the golf course, you discover that every time you swing the club, you get a hole in one. *Every time.* You start using it in competition, and suddenly you're unbeatable. One after another, the top pros topple, including Tiger Woods. You win every tournament with ease.

At first, the experience is thrilling. But after a while, it starts losing its appeal. Now that you know you can't lose, the excitement evaporates. There's no satisfaction, no Light generated, because there is no challenge to overcome. In fact, you start to feel chronically dissatisfied, even a little silly; your life as a pro golfer, which was once so rewarding, now tastes like ashes.

In this scenario, you've been accumulating Bread of Shame. Not only does this feel crummy in the moment, but it gets worse over time. Kabbalistically, you're not building a vessel for the Light. Remember, don't think of this vessel as a bowl or container; in Kabbalah, a vessel is a dynamic field of energy whose size is determined by the actions we take and which allows us to receive and retain fulfillment. Without a vessel, we can't really be filled. And this vessel is formed by the effort of actually earning what we get.

Enabling

a. General enabling

General enabling is another damaging aspect of Bread of Shame. In this case, it's not a matter of us benefitting from something we didn't earn. Instead, it's a matter of our contributing to someone else's Bread of Shame, albeit often unwittingly. If I have a guest in my house who shows no signs of leaving or a boss who's abusive and I'm afraid to raise the subject, the problem has become mine. Now I'm making it easier for my guest or my boss to accumulate Bread of Shame: I'm allowing them to stay in my home or keep me working late every night when they haven't earned that privilege. Now I'm becoming an accomplice to a spiritual crime.

Parents often stumble into this trap. *I love my kids so much that I'll give them whatever they want.* Unfortunately, this approach is a recipe for unhappiness all around. No matter how much you give your children, it won't be enough. They're going to want more. And more. Instead of appreciating what they do get from you, they'll resent you for what you're not giving them. And you'll be responsible for this mess; with the best of intentions, you've ended up doing your children a real disservice. You've enabled their Bread of Shame by giving and giving without asking them to earn it. You have taken away their opportunity to create a vessel to hold their Light.

b. Seeking Approval

A more subtle way we foster Bread of Shame is by seeking approval from others. When we do something just to gain someone else's approval, we're enabling their Bread of Shame because they didn't earn the benefit they get from our action. As a result, whatever we did, however generous it may seem doesn't generate any Light. It's just an expression of our own need, in this case for recognition.

c. Control

Exercising control over other people is another way we enable Bread of Shame. In this case, we're not allowing people to make their own choices, so they can't earn their own Light. And when we allow someone else to assert control over us, we're enabling their Bread of Shame through the same dynamic.

There's a pattern emerging here. Why would we enable someone else's Bread of Shame? Because it serves our personal agenda. At least, we think it does. It's actually just serving our ego, which on a deeper level is working against us, keeping us from evolving as spiritual beings. Like the wife who caters to her husband's need for flattery instead of pointing out where he can do better, when we enable Bread of Shame, we're hurting others as well as ourselves.

Have you ever found it difficult to speak the truth to your best friend for fear that you may be putting the relationship in jeopardy? We've all felt that way at times, even though we know that true friendship is based on both parties being able to share their innermost feelings (note: tact is always helpful here). Friendship is based on being able to speak and hear the truth, even when it's uncomfortable. Otherwise, we're enabling Bread of Shame.

The same principle can be found at work in corporate life. It's tempting to tell your boss what she or he wants to hear, but you can't do that all the time and still keep your integrity. You've got to stand up for what you believe or you'll lose respect for yourself, and eventually your boss will, too. At the end of the day, people recognize the truth and whether they know it or not, the truth is really what they want.

This applies to love relationships as well. My grandmother always said, "The first fight is always the best fight." What she meant by this was that we shouldn't wait for things to come to a boil. That only makes the upcoming argument worse. Be straight. Unfortunately, in love relationships, we often keep the truth from each other for fear of ending up alone. But if a relationship is based on lies or half-truths, isn't it better to know that sooner rather than later? If you bring children into this environment of marital compromise-through-fear, what message are you giving them? You're teaching them to settle. You're teaching them to sleepwalk through life. You're teaching them to perpetuate Bread of Shame.

True sharing, real love cannot include contributing to someone else's Bread of Shame. You can't build a vessel for anyone but yourself; that's how the system works. So look closely at your motivation when you're inclined to give your children whatever they want. Where does that feeling come from? Are you trying to avoid a confrontation? Do you feel guilty that you're not spending more time with your kids? Are you eager to be liked by them? Are you compensating for something your parents didn't do for you?

We've arrived at yet another paradox in Kabbalah. You'd think sharing would always mean giving and in a sense it does, but the sharing we're looking for is a state of consciousness. It's spiritual sharing. Sometimes it requires saying yes, and sometimes it requires saying no. When your three-year-old child wants to cross a busy city street on her own, "no" is the sharing response.

Most people equate sharing with giving, so let's take a closer look at what spiritual sharing really looks like.

Nine Principles of Spiritual Sharing

Principle #1: Becoming a being of sharing does not mean changing other people. True sharing is born of a desire for the other person to get closer to whatever it is that they need.

Principle #2: Give people their space. This is directly related to the previous principle. Giving a person their space means respecting where they are and meeting them there as equals.

Principle #3: Advice is our biggest vice. This is a trap that a lot of people fall into. The best way to share what you've learned is by setting an example of sharing that others may choose to follow.

Principle #4: Have Empathy. You can't resolve other people's issues, but you can share the burden of their pain and thereby lighten it.

Principle #5: Provide unconditional love. Lose your personal agenda. However a relationship serves you, set that aside. If you're upset with someone else, don't say anything for at least three days. Give your soul a chance to make its contribution.

Principle #6: Let yourself off the hook. Remember, you cannot control how things turn out. All you can do is have the right consciousness and then let the Light do its thing.

Principle #7: Have certainty in the Light. When someone comes to you with a problem, your certainty in the Light of the Creator will make itself felt more powerfully than any direction you can provide.

Principle #8: Listen and be present. Often when a person comes to me with a question or a problem, the truth of the matter is that I don't know what that person really needs. So I'll pause, open myself up, and pose the question to the Light. Sometimes I'll get an answer, and sometime I won't. Again, the best thing is just to be there with the person. The simple act of listening to another human being can be incredibly powerful. You're letting yourself be a vessel, which allows the other person to be the Light.

Principle #9: Ask yourself: Am I helping or am I hurting the person I'm with? Helping a person means allowing yourself to be a mirror, allowing that person to see themselves more clearly. You can recognize if you're hurting someone when you offer a suggestion and the person starts arguing with you. The moment this starts happening, you know that there is no vessel for the energy you want to give the person. You've got to go back to the previous principle: Listen, be present, and let that person go through their process.

We can all learn to replace Bread of Shame with genuine sharing. Stay vigilant. Question your motives. As a teacher, I find it all too easy to enable my students and to be enabled by them. After all, I want them to like me. So I work hard to be aware of those pitfalls and to avoid them. It's not easy, but it's well worth the effort.

Rewriting Your Script

Here are three questions I would like you to consider.

1. Where in your life have you tasted Bread of Shame? When have you wanted something and received it without having had to work for it?

2. Where have you enabled Bread of Shame? When have you given other people—especially your children—things they didn't deserve or earn?

3. Where have other people enabled your Bread of Shame? This isn't easy to see, but look for occasions when people have done things for you, but not for the right reasons—not because they really wanted what was best for you.

Think about these three questions. Write your answers out. If you can't readily come up with anything, ask someone you trust to tell you the truth. Ask your best friend, "Are you afraid to tell me things because you're afraid of hurting our friendship?" Ask your parents. Ask your children. Do some digging.

Chapter 5

Meet Your Opponent, The Ego

As your work with Kabbalah starts to bear fruit, at some point you will begin to notice the presence of your ego, or as we call it in The Kabbalah Centre, the voice of the Opponent. This is the prideful facet of yourself that resists change and defends things as they are. Early on in your spiritual journey, the Opponent may not show up. But as you really start to make progress, at some point you'll confront the Opponent face-to-face. And this is actually a good sign.

When we start our spiritual work, the Opponent doesn't take us seriously. After all, how often do people follow through on what they've begun? How many times do we start diets and not stick to them, or join a gym and stop going after the first few weeks? But when the Opponent sees that we're not giving up, he reassesses the situation and steps in. So when we see our Opponent, we know we're making progress. We know we're moving forward.

What is the purpose of this Opponent? The Creator introduced the Opponent to keep the game of life from being too easy. The Opponent provides the resistance we need to bring down the Light. Without the Opponent, we would all suffer Bread of Shame. Without the Opponent, we could never move to the next spiritual level.

The *Zohar*—a commentary on the Torah or Bible, and the foundational work in the literature of Kabbalah—explains that from the moment we come out of the womb, the Opponent attaches to us to push us to greatness, to help us connect to lasting fulfillment. In this way, obstacles are truly opportunities in disguise. Kabbalistically, mistakes are only mistakes if we don't learn from them. When we fall down in our spiritual work, we'll know better how to overcome the Opponent the next time.

This is not to say that the Opponent isn't formidable. Quite the contrary. He's tireless. While we're sleeping, he's working hard to come up with ways to trigger our reactivity, shame, and depression. The Opponent has been around a long time—since the creation of the world, in fact—and he's very clever. Without the Light, we wouldn't stand a chance against him. We simply could not fight our way through the obstacles he poses.

Our ego, which is home territory for the Opponent, is like a mask covering the soul. Our problems begin when we forget this and start to identify ourselves with the ego. We allow ourselves to become driven by selfish desires, and we begin to block and cover over our soul's connection to the Light.

Technology for the Soul

At The Kabbalah Centre, we provide many different outreach programs where we teach Kabbalah to various communities around the world, including prisons. One of the places we've done this work is Riker's Island in New York City. Situated on a little island in the East River, Riker's is one of the largest prisons in the world, home to more than 30,000 inmates.

Maintaining the mask of ego isn't so easily done in prison. It's harder to pretend to yourself that everything is okay. This strips away a lot of pretense, allowing some prison inmates a degree of openness and humility that might be more difficult to achieve in the outside world. So ironically, we who live outside prison walls can be more spiritually constrained than some involuntary tenants of Riker's Island. They've come to terms with who they are.

As you read this, you might well ask yourself, *What kind of mask do I have on right now? How have I become imprisoned by my own ego? How has it contributed to my victim-consciousness?* The saying "Keep your friends close, and your enemies closer" also applies to the ego. Our first step is to recognize the ego and then to observe it closely. We need to understand how it works so it doesn't run the show without any input from our soul.

As we've seen, one useful way of looking at the ego is to understand that it unknowingly provides us with a map of the negativity inside us. If you listen to the ego while maintaining your awareness that it's not really who you are, you can use it to reveal the internal issues that you need to work on.

This leads us to a more nuanced understanding of how the ego works, which is very exciting. We're seeing not just the revealed ego but also the concealed ego, which hides behind our public persona. To take an astrological example, Scorpios can feel fragile inside themselves, so they tend to overcompensate by displaying anger or by seeking to control the situation (you'll find more on astrology in

Chapter 13). As we learn to work with the ego, we find that our inner landscape is not what the exterior would lead us to believe.

Revealing Concealed Ego

Let's use an exercise to explore this idea of the ego having multiple levels. Below you'll see 12 different manifestations of ego: Rage, anger, depression, sadness, etc. I'd like you to number them in terms of their importance in your life, from one to twelve, one being the highest and most important, twelve being the lowest and least important.

For instance, if you think rage is not an issue for you at all, that is a #12. It's the least of your problems. And if you think that the desire for control is your #1 issue, meaning the problem you most need to work on, then give it a #1.

Revealed / Concealed Ego

Fill this out as truthfully as you possibly can. If you're reading a library book, make a copy of this page and fill that out, so other readers can do this exercise, too. Remember that there are no right or wrong answers, and that all of us grapple with the ego on a regular basis.

1. Note the following 12 aspects of the ego:

___ Rage
___ Being defensive
___ Judgment
___ Pride
___ Depression
___ Desire to control

___ Being inconsiderate

___ Disconnecting from people

___ Being vengeful (carrying grudges)

___ Jealousy

___ Taking others for granted

___ Being abrasive or hostile

2. Rate the aspects of ego:

    a. Find the aspect of the ego you relate to the most and place #1 next to it.

    b. Write this #1 aspect here. _____

    c. Look for the ego aspect that you relate to the least. Put #12 beside that one.

    d. Write your #12 aspect here. _____

    e. Rate the rest from most to least.

Now that you've assigned a number to each issue that you need to work on, look at that list carefully. Take a look at what you chose as your #1 ego issue. This is your visible expression of ego. Kabbalah teaches us that what you've put down as #12, the aspect you think is not your issue, is actually your cause ego. It's your concealed ego, the part of you that needs to be dealt with but is hidden by your mask. A lot of us don't want to go there for fear of what we may find. But the truth is always less scary than our fears.

Our Biggest Problems Are the Hardest to Find

According to my father's spiritual teacher, Rav Brandwein, what we focus on is often not what's important. And what we don't focus on is often *very* important. When someone is hot-tempered, all we see is a hostile person, when really all that person may want is to be loved. Our ego likes to play this game with us, distracting us with surface impressions to keep us from seeing the truth, both in our own lives and in the lives of others.

From a kabbalistic perspective, the more things are concealed, the closer they are to the truth; the more they are revealed, the further from the truth they are. In World War II, when Generals Montgomery and Eisenhower were planning to invade Normandy, they leaked fake documents to the Germans indicating they were going to land farther north. Their ruse succeeded in diverting crucial military resources from the beaches where the Allied landing craft actually came ashore.

Our ego is doing this all the time, creating diversionary tactics so that we mistake the source of the problem. The external ego is a diversion. It's the concealed, or internal, ego that needs the real work.

Rewrite Your Script

Take a few minutes to focus on the #12 ego issue that you listed above, the one you considered to be your least important ego problem. Think about it and write down your thoughts. Consider where in your life this issue may be affecting you most. Your #12 may have been depression, or rage, or the desire to control others. Try hard to find places where that issue may be showing up in your life. Ask other people what they think, too. You may be surprised by what you find.

Chapter 6

Ego Hide and Seek

If you don't get to the cause, if you don't find the concealed ego aspect at work in your life, what happens? You may move on to another issue and work really hard at it, only to find that, once again, you're not seeing any results. Why? Because you're just skating along the surface. If you just keep on dealing with your #1 or #2 issues, all you're going to be doing is exchanging one external problem for another. And you're never going to get to the root cause.

Our Issues Are Reflected in the People around Us

There was a time when the phrase "going postal" was in wide circulation. The term derived from several cases where postal workers came to work with guns and went on mass killing sprees, but it pointed to a larger cultural phenomenon. People were becoming so angry at work that their feelings boiled over into terrible acts of violence. According to Kabbalah, you can suppress feelings for only so long before they explode.

The only way to prevent feelings from getting out of hand is to stop hiding them away where they will only grow in power. Expose them to the light of day. Nothing and no one is immune to this basic principle. You could call this the ultimate game of hide-and-seek, with the ego being that kid who always seemed to discover the one nook or cranny where no one would find him. If we keep on just paying attention to the externals *(I went to church or synagogue or mosque and I prayed so I have transformed)*, we won't make the deeper spiritual connection that can change our lives.

The story of Jacob and the angel in the Book of Genesis offers us a clue to this spiritual principle. Jacob and the angel are fighting, and Jacob wins the battle. He then asks the angel, "What is your name?" and the angel replies, "Why do you want to know my name?" Kabbalists wonder why Jacob was so interested in the name of the angel. And why was the angel so crafty in his reply, which divulged nothing?

Jacob represents the Light, and the angel represents the Opponent, the ego. When Jacob asks for the name of the angel, he's really asking, "Where is your hiding place? How can I reveal you to those who come after me?" The angel's answer reveals the secret that as long as we don't know his name (in Kabbalah, a name is a code or connection to the essence of a person), we cannot win the battle. For what we see of a person—the ego—is just a conjurer's trick. There's really nothing there.

Like the magician sawing his assistant in half, once you know how it's done, the trick loses its power. Once you expose the source of the anger that's causing your various external conflicts, for instance, you can defuse it. You see that its power is simply based on fantasies, on stories you've been telling yourself all your life. Unfortunately, we buy into the ego most of the time. But as we come to learn more about its nature, when we can name it, the ego's hold on us starts to weaken.

The great 18th century kabbalist, the Baal Shem Tov, was known for channeling Light to make miraculous changes in people's lives. After visiting him, women unable to have children miraculously gave birth, and people who were poor suddenly found financial fortune.

The Baal Shem Tov taught that other people provide one of the best ways to find the root cause of our own ego, especially in those moments when they're pushing our buttons. That's when they're revealing our ego at its hidden, causal level. Instead of looking inside ourselves, we often prefer to project the cause of our stormy feelings onto the other person. *I'm never going to forgive him because he has hurt me.* The truth is just the opposite: That person is really a messenger from the Light, showing us where our ego resides. Other people are mirrors, reflecting back the truth of what lies deep inside us.

Re-Working the Ego

One way to deal with the terrific resistance we often put up when someone else serves as a mirror to us is to be grateful. *Thank you for what you've shown me, and how can I help you in return?* When you do this, you'll find to your astonishment that other people will stop upsetting you. While it may seem as if suddenly the upsetting people around you have changed, this is really just a reflection of the shift taking place inside you.

It gets even better. Once you've made a commitment to put your ego in harm's way, the promise of Kabbalah is that the people around you really *will* start to change. Your newly elevated consciousness is going to extend into their lives. And that's the way we thank those people who act as mirrors for us. It's a beautiful process of give-and-take, one from which everyone benefits.

This reminds me of two brothers I know quite well, both of whom were very successful in business. They started studying at The Kabbalah Centre, and it quickly became obvious that they were fiercely competitive with each other. One of the brothers evolved a great deal through his work at The Centre, but the other didn't take his studies as seriously and made less progress.

The one who worked harder sorted through a lot of pain and improved his life significantly, but the one area that resisted improvement was his relationship with his brother. Eventually, however, after he brought to the surface his belief that he wasn't as good as his brother, he was able to change even further. To his surprise, when he no longer felt competitive with his brother, his brother stopped dumping on him. Once that button wasn't being pushed, the two brothers developed a great relationship, and the second brother was inspired to work harder to sort out his own issues. Things between them changed just because one of them changed.

The lesson here is that you don't need two to do the transformation tango. If you change yourself, the people around you may not necessarily transform, too, but at the very least, *they'll change in relationship to you.* Don't fall into the trap of thinking that you can fix the other people in your life. We can't change anyone else. We can only hope to change ourselves. But in changing ourselves, we can still transform our relationships. When we rewrite the role that our character performs, the entire script changes to accommodate it.

A Tale of Transformation

There was once a young married couple that didn't have any children, although they had tried for a long time. After many inquiries, they learned of a kabbalist and healer in a distant village whom they hoped might give them a blessing so they could have a child. The husband set out on the long journey to meet the kabbalist and finally arrived at the address he'd been given. The house was so small and dilapidated that he checked his directions several times to be sure he'd come to the right place. *This can't be the home of a great sage,* he thought to himself.

When he knocked on the door, a disheveled man in shabby clothes opened it. Behind him, several equally ragged children were playing on the floor. The traveler was so surprised by this sight that he just stood in the doorway, speechless. After waiting a few seconds for his visitor to speak, the kabbalist shut the door.

The young husband didn't know what to do. He had traveled far, and he didn't want to return home without being able to give his wife new hope. So he found a nearby barn to sleep in, then spent the next week considering the reasons for his journey so that the next time he wouldn't be so inarticulate. He looked inside himself unflinchingly and explored each of his issues in depth, allowing himself to get in touch with the innermost thoughts and feelings that drove his behavior.

But when he went back to the kabbalist's home, the same thing happened. The traveler was again struck dumb by the slovenly scene and couldn't get beyond being judgmental; and once again the kabbalist closed the door on him. After another week, the young man tried again, and again he was rebuffed. Finally, after three solid weeks of scouring his soul, he made a fourth attempt to meet the kabbalist.

This time, he couldn't believe his eyes. The same house looked cozy and welcoming. What had happened to the shack he'd seen before? The kabbalist seemed knowing and kind, and his children were bright and well behaved.

As he looked around the little cottage, the traveler suddenly realized that he no longer needed to ask the kabbalist for help. After the weeks of working on his issues, the world now looked so different to him that he understood he had achieved his mission himself. And sure enough, nine months after he returned home, the traveler and his wife were blessed with a child.

This story illuminates where our real work needs to take place. The ego filters our experiences, selecting only the bits and pieces that fit our preconceived ideas and our stories, many of which are negative and judgmental. But when we tackle the core beliefs and feelings of our ego and trace them to their roots, we change our perspective, which changes everything.

* * *

In this chapter, we've seen how the ego hides from our conscious awareness and that we need to find it to learn how it works. One of the best ways to do this is to look at the kinds of behavior that trigger us, behaviors we find mirrored back to us by people we find upsetting. Once we do locate the hidden residence of the ego, its power over us dissipates.

If you're struggling with the idea that the people who push your buttons are actually just reflecting your own deep internal workings, let's imagine that someone is standing right in front of you driving you crazy. The person is trying to control you, for example, demanding that you do this or that, and that you do it now. You're starting to feel like a victim, and you're getting angry, so how could this person possibly be showing you something important about yourself?

Try turning this quality that's upsetting you around on yourself. *How do I try to control other people or situations in my life?* If you can't see it, take a closer look. Perhaps it's not obvious. Perhaps you exert control through a feeling of entitlement, or by expecting too much from other people, or by judging them unfairly.

Sometimes, what the person is showing you is not how you behave but how your consciousness operates in terms of your relationship with the Light. By understanding your own motivation, you might become clearer about the motivation of others and be capable of navigating the relationship differently. Keep asking the question: *What am I supposed to learn from this?* Ask the Light to reveal the lesson to expand your soul.

This process does not apply, however, to severe emotional, mental, or physical abuse. Cases of abuse have their own lessons to teach us. Often, we need to learn to respect and protect the Light within ourselves and not give anyone permission to cover it over with their actions or their words. Such extreme circumstances require more than this book offers. What I recommend as a first step in your efforts to rewrite that movie is to decide to seek help. Your ego may be telling you that it's okay for someone to hurt you because you don't deserve better but your soul sees it differently. The help of a professional can help you separate yourself from the abuse and the abuser, and begin to reveal your Light.

Rewriting Your Script

This chapter's exercise won't be easy, but it will be rewarding. Select a person you trust and ask them what they think your ego reveals about you. Request that they be completely honest. No holding back. For your part, you have to promise not to respond to what they say, but simply to write down the information you're being given. If you really want to stretch yourself, go to someone who has upset you lately, perhaps someone with whom you're angry but whom you fundamentally trust, and ask them to go through this process with you. This is really putting yourself on the line, but by doing so, you'll learn a tremendous amount about how your ego is triggered.

* * *

If you'd like to do more work on people who push your buttons, turn to the Appendix, where you'll find that the third of the three exercises there directly relates to this topic.

Chapter 7

Passing Judgment

Judgment has evolutionary importance as a critical faculty: If our ancestors hadn't been able to make the right choice when faced with a saber-toothed tiger, or Tyrannosaurus Rex, our genes wouldn't have been passed on to the next generation. But this same capacity can also create separation between us and our children, our parents, and whomever else we've judged, and into that resulting space can enter anger, hatred, and all sorts of destructive emotions. When we look at someone we're judging harshly, we see everything they do as wrong, and this feeling builds and builds until we can no longer make a meaningful connection with that person.

Judgment is the Opponent's single most powerful tool. By the time we finish judging someone, we can be so worked up that we can't even remember the original cause of the problem. And it's just a quick hop from judgment to discrimination to hatred, one of the most toxic feelings in the human repertoire.

Judgment is so central to the human experience—and so potentially dangerous—that one of the kabbalistic laws of the universe is devoted to it. When we act destructively by passing judgment on others, the universe in turn will pass judgment on us. We've created negative energy that will eventually come back to us. It's as if there is a conduit in the universe through which all judgments pass: For judgment to come down on us, we need to open that pipe, and we open the pipe when we judge others. But if we keep the pipe closed, no judgment can befall us. Simply put, the universe cannot judge us until we judge somebody else. So if we live our life maybe not perfectly but at least without passing judgment, no negative energy can be visited on us. If the only thing you learn is how not to judge others harshly, you can have a fulfilling life.

The Story of the Beggar and the Baker

This story takes place in the town of Safed, where the great kabbalist Isaac Luria lived.

One day, the local baker wakes up and decides he would like to bring more spirituality into his life, so he asks his wife, "How can we strengthen our connection to the Creator? We're not rich and all we know is our humble craft, yet there must be something we can do."

That night, the baker takes up a sack filled with loaves of bread and sets out to see how he can make a larger connection to the Light. He sees a house of study, walks in, and begins to pray. "God, I just want to find a way to serve You. I want to give You something in return for the goodness You've shown me, for the satisfying life You've given me, my wife, and my children." He sets down his offering of bread, rises, and walks home through the dark streets.

Not long after, a beggar enters the same house of study. He, too, prays. "God, I have nothing. My family is starving. I am desperate, and I have no place else to turn." He begins to weep. Heavy-hearted, he is preparing to leave when he notices the baker's sack stuffed with loaves of bread. Filled with gratitude, he says, "God, I thank You for hearing my prayer," and runs home, knowing that on this night at least, his family can eat their fill.

The following night, the baker returns to the house of study and sees that his bread is no longer there. Delighted, he goes home and tells his wife, "Let's bake some more. God has accepted our gift of gratitude, so let's replenish it." He returns to the house of the study with more fresh loaves, thanks the Creator, and leaves. Not long after, the beggar walks in and offers up another prayer. Sure enough, when he's finished, he looks around and finds another large paper sack filled with bread.

This exchange takes place every night for the next 15 years.

One day, the proprietor of the house of study stays up unusually late and is surprised to hear a man's voice in the sanctuary. When he goes to investigate, he overhears the town's baker praying, then sees him set down a large bag and leave. Shortly thereafter, a beggar comes in, prays silently for a few minutes, then takes the bag the baker left behind and goes on his way.

The next morning, the proprietor sends a servant to summon both the beggar and the baker. To the baker he says, "Last night, I overheard your prayer, and I must inform you that, contrary to your belief, God has not chosen to visit a humble baker. The loaves of bread you are leaving here are being eaten by this beggar." And to the beggar he says, "There is no God in this house for you. The loaves you have come here to receive are the work of this man, a mere baker."

Rav Isaac Luria, studying unnoticed nearby, comes over to the proprietor of the house of study and says, "You need to prepare yourself, good sir. You're going to leave this world today." Stunned, the proprietor asks why. The rabbi replies, "When you saw the baker leave his loaves, you said to yourself, 'He's a fool for thinking his gift of bread can be meaningful to the Creator.' Then, when you saw the beggar, you thought, 'He's a fool, too; he actually thinks God is giving him bread.'"

"Unfortunately, by passing judgment you have disrupted the perfect circuitry of Light being created in your house of study. Fifteen years ago, you were supposed to leave this world, but these two men—one in his simple desire to serve the Creator and the other in his humble certainty that the Creator was indeed taking care of him—generated so much Light that your life was protected. Now that you have brought this circuitry to an end, the judgment of the universe that was meant for you can be postponed no longer."

When we judge others, we shatter our own shield of protection and allow judgment to be visited on us.

Seeking Judgment

Imagine for a moment that you're walking down the street, minding your own business. Somebody bumps into you hard. You turn around in anger, only to find that the offender is a blind man, tapping his white cane on the sidewalk. All the judgment you were poised to unleash *(How can you be so clumsy?)* evaporates. What happened in that split second? Thanks to a shift in consciousness, you replaced judgment with compassion.

The more you are willing to explore how judgmental you're being, the more quickly you're going to be able to let these feelings go. Unfortunately, simply suppressing judgmental feelings doesn't work.

As we've seen, suppression creates a space that results in separation between people, which is almost as bad as judgment itself. The only way to really get rid of judgment is to bring it to the surface and then put yourself in the other person's shoes.

Rewriting Your Script

Consider a time when you reacted strongly to someone in your life. Now sit down and write a letter to that person, giving voice to all the reasons you were upset, hurt, or angry. Don't hold anything back. Give all those emotions a full airing. Don't mail this letter, just use it to express your feelings. When those feelings have dissipated, return to the letter and reread it.

Consider these questions. Were you in a reactive space when you wrote the letter? Were you coming from a place of judgment? How might you proactively intervene when moments like this happen in the future? As Jack Nicholson says in *A Few Good Men*, "You can't handle the truth." But his character was just rationalizing his own bad behavior. You *can* handle the truth. Be honest with yourself. The more honest you are, the more you will benefit from this exercise.

Chapter 8

Fear and Uncertainty

Having seen all the woes that ego creates in our lives, why do we cling to it so desperately? Why is it so difficult to challenge the ego's hegemony?

There are two major reasons. Either we are unaware of the ego as a separate entity and therefore confuse it with the self, or we hold on to it out of fear. Our ego can seem like a faithful friend, even if it is high-maintenance. It's the known. It's what we've grown used to. It lulls us with its familiar refrain: *Don't worry, we'll get through this together.*

It's as if we were a lobster, and the ego is the water in the pot. If we were dropped into boiling water, we'd try to scramble out. But if you put us into room-temperature water and slowly turned up the heat, we'd adjust to each new hike in temperature without complaint. We'd succumb to our fate without trying to escape.

Fear is part of our hardwiring. Deep in the limbic system of the brain lie the mechanisms for the fight-or-flight response. When we're faced with a threat, the body responds in one of two ways: Either by preparing to do battle with the enemy or by preparing to flee so we can live to fight another day. One of the interesting aspects of this response is that it can't distinguish between a real threat and an imagined one. In both cases, we get the same jolt of adrenaline, our blood flow diverts to our major muscles, and we go on high alert.

This fight-or-flight response has obvious survival benefits. It's great when we're facing a real external threat—a mugger, a drunk driver, a belligerent bar patron—but it's far less useful when someone at work is evaluating our performance, or we're stuck in traffic, or we're looking at a shockingly high credit card bill. In the latter cases, when we respond to stress with the ancient response of preparing to fight or flee, we're more likely to add to the problem. We react defensively to criticism, for example, instead of investigating its merits or we're likely to cut off the aggressive driver as a form of payback.

Fear is one of the tools the ego uses to stay in control, keeping us hooked to its constant stream of advice on how best to survive. This makes fear the enemy of our soul's mission to engage in spiritual growth. Kabbalah teaches us that if we're charting our life journey based on fear, we're just going to generate chaos. When we allow fear to run our lives, we become our own worst enemy. It's a self-fulfilling prophecy.

* * *

This exercise may sound odd, but give it a try. Look at yourself in the mirror and say the following words out loud: "I am filled with Light, I am powerful. I can accomplish anything I truly wish to do." Look right into your eyes, as you would a friend, and repeat these sentences three times. At first, you'll probably sound tentative. After all, this is a big claim, and most of us struggle with less than stellar self-esteem. But when you think about it, you can find places in your life where you've felt full of Light—powerful, confident, and certain. Tap into those places now, and go back to the mirror again.

Repeat these sentences three more times. This time around you may find your performance more convincing. And part of you is no longer acting; it really accepts these statements as true (which, of course, they are). Continue with this exercise for several more rounds. Check in with your body along the way. Are you beginning to feel less uncomfortable? Are you beginning to relax into the truth of these statements?

I'd like you to incorporate this moment into your day on a regular basis. It's certainly convenient enough, given that most people start and end the day in the bathroom. This gives you at least two good opportunities each day to go several rounds with these consciousness-raising statements. How much time do most of us spend making critical observations about ourselves? Let's make a small effort to redress the balance by making positive observations that are much more in tune with reality.

Doubt versus Certainty

Kabbalah has a one-word response to the array of tricks that the ego plays on us. And that word is *certainty*. Not to be confused with arrogance, certainty is more like justifiable confidence, as in: "I do this because I know it will bring me fulfillment in the future." The more certainty you have, the more power you possess to bring that positive future towards you and the more effective you'll be at negotiating the negative forces that stand in your way.

If you think about what drives fear, it's uncertainty about the future. When you're aware, however, that the Lightforce of the Creator is all around you, surrounding and protecting you, your fears evaporate. Did you ever see the movie *Oh, God!* with George Burns? In the film, God is walking around in the body of George Burns. Imagine being a friend of his, knowing that God is walking right next to you all the time. Would you ever fear anything? It's only when we doubt the presence of the Light in a given situation that we make room for fear.

Kabbalists tell us that if we don't fill a space with Light, it's going to get filled with darkness. Moreover, that's going to encourage us to make decisions that attract more darkness. So what's the answer? Injecting certainty into our consciousness. And how do we do that? Paradoxically, we use equal measures of doubt and personal experience:

1. Doubt the doubt that you're having. Doubt your fears. In this way, you use the weapons of the ego against itself.

2. Become more aware of the Light. The Light always wins. It banishes darkness every time. As you experience this more and more, you will awaken your certainty in the Lightforce of the Creator and in the 99% Realm.

Rewriting Your Script

Sit down with a pencil and a piece of paper, and jot down your fears. Not your infrequent worries, but the fears that affect you on a daily basis. Then pick a big one—a chronic fear, perhaps even a debilitating fear. Sit with it. Summon the feelings associated with the fear. Write them down, and then just be with them.

At first, they may seem unbearable but stay with this process, breathing deeply into the places where your body tightens up. It won't be long before the fear passes because fear is a feeling and feelings pass. When you are done, take the piece of paper with its description of this fear over to the sink and burn it.

Now write about this experience in detail. In a few days, try going through the same process with another fear. Bit by bit, you'll feel the burden of your fears begin to lighten.

Chapter 9

Addiction

We are all addicts. We all have something we're addicted to, whether it is food, shopping, alcohol, sex, drugs, control, or anything else we constantly crave. How does this happen?

The answer lies in the cycle of souls. Just as we choose our parents as part of the process of working through our *tikkun*, our soul's correction, we also come into this world with addictions that help to underscore the need for that work. How do we know what we need to correct? Whatever we're addicted to. Even more forcefully than our problems with our ego, our addictions tell us where our garbage is, so we can clean it up. Once recognized, addiction is an arrow pointing to what we need to address in our consciousness.

Addictions are based on genuine needs; in fact, they derive from five basic psychological and spiritual needs we all share:

1. to feel loved and cared for,
2. to give love,
3. to belong,
4. to express ourselves creatively, and

5. to bring the Lightforce of the Creator into our lives (this need contains all our other needs, just as the Light contains everything that exists within it).

We turn to addiction as a way of filling one or more of these basic requirements. But when we do so, all we're settling for is a hollow imitation of the real thing. What we really want is Light but we settle for food or alcohol because we can get those right away, which has tremendous appeal when our desire is so strong. That's the source of our drive towards addiction. We all want Light but we don't know how to get it, so we settle for what we can get right now.

The Rav, my father and co-founder of The Kabbalah Centre, once wrote that substance abusers are insightful enough to appreciate that there's more to life than mundane existence, than the 1%. They're right, and in this way they're attuned to the voice of the soul. The problem with addiction is not that it's immoral but that it doesn't work. If being addicted made people happy long-term, it would be great. As the Rav once said, if scientists could invent a pill that kept us happy for the rest of our life, he'd be the first person in line to take it. The problem with addiction is that the price for its temporary fulfillment is long-term pain.

What Lies Beneath

In truth, there are two kinds of addictions. There are the more obvious physical addictions (to smoking, drugs, sex, alcohol, shopping, work, etc.). Then there are the invisible emotional addictions, which are even more pervasive than the physical ones; in fact, they plague each and every one of us. They include the need for control, for recognition, and for comfort. Some people are addicted to drama and will create it when daily life doesn't provide enough. Others are addicted to anger or to being judgmental. Compared to physical addictions, emotional addictions are more difficult to find and tougher to fix.

I think more people are addicted to approval than anything else, even coffee (and I know how much I crave my Starbucks in the morning). Often, we don't see the lengths we go to in order to satisfy emotional addiction, nor do we notice the damage this subtler kind of addiction wreaks on us and on those around us. We can't take an MRI and see the effect of chronic anger in the same way we can scan someone's lungs to see the impact on them of 20 years of smoking.

Perhaps the most difficult thing about addiction is that half measures don't work. The only way to attain fulfillment if you're an addict is to stop being an addict. The addiction itself can never be satisfied. You can never drink enough alcohol if you're an alcoholic; you can never achieve enough control if you're a control freak. If an addict wants his or her vessel filled, he or she needs to turn away from the addiction and go for the real thing.

Ego plays a huge role in emotional addiction. It puts us in need of recognition and approval, of controlling or being controlled. The ego feeds these needs with feelings of unworthiness or insecurity, with fears of abandonment or embarrassment. We have gold available to us in the Light, but we settle for lead—and then wonder why we feel so dissatisfied. Instead of listening to the quiet, knowing voice of our soul deep inside us, we pin our hope for happiness on people and things in the outside world.

I used to be very overweight, and much of that was based on shutting down my feelings. In my case, I'd sit in front of the TV and eat, barely registering how much food I was wolfing down. I think this lack of consciousness is at work in lots of addictions, so breaking the addiction begins with an awareness of our underlying thoughts and feelings, followed by specific steps (in my case, I decided I could only eat in the kitchen) to raise our consciousness to a new level and to direct our actions from there.

Addiction is a metaphor for life. To have the life we want, we also have to become aware and then make a shift in consciousness. It's the only way to rewrite our movie.

I have a close friend who's in a love relationship but it's not bringing out the best in either him or his partner. How does this manifest day to day? Well, instead of being involved with other people, my friend is enmeshed in his relationship to the exclusion of everything else.

I finally succeeded in taking him out to dinner, but my friend spent the entire evening texting his girlfriend. This inability to connect with other people in a genuine way is a classic sign of addiction. I spoke to my friend about it, but with no effect. This raises an important point. How do you deal with a friend or family member that's caught up in an addiction? What can you do?

From a kabbalistic perspective, we know that we can't fix anyone else; we can only fix ourselves. Unfortunately, many of us need to hit bottom before we start to find our way back. I'm hoping that we don't have to get to that point, but all too often, that turns out to be the case.

Idol Worship and Slavery

According to the *Zohar*, addiction is a form of both idol worship and slavery. This doesn't refer to the idols that the Greeks and Romans prayed to or to the golden calf in the Bible. Kabbalistically, idol worship takes place any time we pursue something other than the Light. Chasing after temporary fulfillment is idol worship.

When we place another person above us, when we give them power over us, when we seek their approval, that's idol worship and slavery. We're making that person the source of our happiness. We've just created a god—a false god—to serve.

This is why Kabbalah is careful not to make itself about any one individual. At The Kabbalah Centre, we have lots of kabbalistic scholars, we teach many courses, and we train many teachers. My father, my mother, my brother, and I work with a team of talented people, and we all run The Centre together. Kabbalists respect and even admire their teachers but we do not put them above us.

Why are kabbalists so careful to do this? Because we recognize that the ego is waiting to ensnare us, to create a need in us for something external in order to be happy—an idol to worship. But there is only one source of fulfillment—the Light. And the Light can only be found by overcoming obstacles as we shift our consciousness from the Desire to Share for Selfish Reasons to the Desire to Share for the Benefit of All.

One of the reasons religion causes so much pain and suffering in the world is that it becomes about either the teacher or the religious system itself as the interpreter of God's will. But God is not out there. God is inside us. This's where we have to look for fulfillment. Looking anywhere else opens the door to idol worship and slavery.

Rewriting Your Script

Now I'm going to ask you to let go of your preconceptions about addiction. It isn't just about that guy who drinks too much or that girl who takes too many drugs. Set that notion aside. Instead, ask yourself where you see a pattern of addictive behavior in your own life. Ask yourself these questions: Where am I addicted to approval from another person? Where do I let something else become more important to me than my soul's connection to the Light? Am I a sex hound? A junkie for attention? Am I addicted to being in control?

Try the following exercise. Arrange some time (say, between six and twelve hours) that you can spend in silence. During this period, you won't be saying a word to anyone. The planning required to find this time is part of the exercise.

The precise length of time is up to you. What matters is that you're making a conscious decision to shut down an important 1% function for the sake of elevating your consciousness. Self-control is normally absent in the addictive dynamic, which is why this exercise is so effective. By giving up an important daily activity, you will prove to yourself that you can reassert this self-control. It's okay. The Light will take care of what you need.

Part Three
Tools for Transformation

Chapter 10

The Energy of Miracles

Have you ever wondered where your thoughts come from? This might sound like a silly question, but why is it that some people have incredible ideas that inspire them to help countless people, while others have dark thoughts that lead them to commit murder? Is it just luck or genetics that leads this person to one kind of thought and that person to another?

Neuroscientists are still far from finding the source of our thoughts, but the ancient kabbalists, who studied this process for thousands of years, believed that thoughts do not actually reside in the brain. Instead, there is an infinite sea of thoughts and ideas available to the brain—a sea that the brain can draw from as needed, a little like today's cloud computing. Kabbalah is not alone in this insight. Hindu philosophy refers to the Akashic records, a field that contains all the information in the universe—past, present, and future. And psychologist Carl Jung, for his part, spoke of the collective consciousness as a sea of thought and energy that we all tap into.

Imagine for a moment that there are only two radio stations in the universe. One is WKAOS (Chaos FM) and the other is KLITE (Light

FM). You're tuned in to either Chaos or Light at any given moment, depending on your consciousness (which is different from your thoughts). Your consciousness determines which of the thoughts that are already out there in the universe you're going to draw down.

From a kabbalistic perspective, any thought that comes into your mind depends on what you're inviting in at that precise moment in time. For example, if you're angry, you're going to invite in thoughts that support more anger. If you are depressed, you're going to bring more sad thoughts into your awareness. On the other hand, if you're focused on personal transformation, tolerance, and compassion, these are the kinds of thoughts you're going to draw down.

Think of the universe as this amazing database of thoughts and energy, and wherever your consciousness is, you're going to download similar thoughts. In more general terms, they're either chaos or Light; choosing between them is the only decision a person ever really makes. Everything else derives from that choice.

When you focus on tuning your antenna to the Light, you're much less likely to hone in on thoughts that contribute to depression, sadness, anxiety, or apathy. When you do, remember that you have the power to change stations. You can't choose who comes to your house, but you can choose who you let in, and the same is true of your mind.

This is a whole new way of thinking about thinking. Up until now, you probably thought that you have no control over the thoughts that enter your consciousness; that it is like a cork bobbing on the surface of the ocean. But now you can see that your mindset and what it chooses to let in are the deciding factors. Once again, you're in the director's chair.

The 99%

When your consciousness is attuned to your soul, you're moving into the 99% Realm, the source of miracles. Where do our off-the-wall creative thoughts come from? They come from the universe. They come from the 99%. On the other hand, if you keep your thoughts in the 1%, don't be surprised if chaos rules your life. *What am I going to have for breakfast? What am I going to have for lunch? What am I going to wear today? Me, me, me, me.*

So does this mean we shouldn't take care of ourselves? Of course not. Even the most mundane things can be used as vehicles for sharing and for miracles. You're going to have breakfast? Who else might need a friendly meal that you could invite over? How about a donation of time or money to your local food bank? When you're getting dressed in the morning, look at all those clothes you never wear and think about donating them to the local charity thrift shop. Everything, no matter how mundane, is an opportunity to elevate your consciousness and that of others.

Special Openings

Did you ever have the feeling that a specific kind of energy seems to predominate in the world around you at certain times? Doesn't it seem as if there are times when lots of people around you are depressed, or getting sick, or having good things happen to them? According to Kabbalah, you've tuned into something important. The universe makes certain energies available at specific times. For example, there is a time during the week when the spiritual realm is more accessible: The 24-hour period between sundown on Friday and sundown on Saturday, known to Jews as the Sabbath. This time, however, isn't a religiously designated occurrence; it's based on the energy of the cosmos. When you understand it this way, it becomes clear that this energy isn't limited to any one religious group, but rather, is available to everyone.

During this time, more Light is available, so try to make the most of it. Spend it with friends, sharing, having dinner together, taking positive actions, talking about spiritual work, reflecting inwardly. Although the Light is always there for us, there are specific windows of time when we can draw down aspects of Light using our consciousness as the receiver, and it's very helpful to know what these special times are so we can take advantage of them.

You can be successful in your spiritual work without connecting to the energy of the Sabbath, but this particular time is a bonus because the energies available are so special. So take some time on this day to meditate, to connect, and to study. Read from the *Zohar*. This is a day when we can bypass Bread of Shame and access the energy of miracles with far less effort than usual. This is a great time to alleviate some of the heavy load of stress that we all tend to carry.

Keep in mind that ritual without consciousness (that is, without a receiver) can't bring us the Light we are looking for. On the other hand, when we bring awareness to ritual, we transform it from mindless to mindful. The underlying reason we participate in a spiritual service is to receive the energy and Light of the Creator. We can attend the most inspiring service at church or synagogue or mosque, but without the consciousness of why we're there, we cannot receive the spiritual nourishment we seek. Add consciousness and we can transform a routine experience into manna for the soul.

According to the *Zohar*, the accomplishments of great sages also create spiritual openings in the cosmos, pulling aside the curtains that separate this world from the realm of Light. These openings allow us to more easily draw that energy into our own lives and accelerate our work. The righteous blaze a trail for those who come after them, so we all have an opportunity to use the energy that they revealed in the universe to assist us in our own changes.

The famous kabbalist Rabbi Akiva spent the first 40 years of his life behaving badly, treating others with lack of dignity, regard, or respect. The *Zohar*, the original text of Kabbalah and the source of all that we teach at The Kabbalah Centre, says that when a righteous person would walk by Rabbi Akiva, he felt the desire to bite that person the way a donkey crushes bones with its jaw. The amazing thing is that even after living this way for 40 years, Rabbi Akiva was able to completely rewrite his script. Though he started his life hating people, he had become a beloved and revered teacher with more than 24,000 students by the time of his death.

The gravesite of a righteous person provides a portal where we can access all the Light and energy that this powerful soul revealed in the world. This is the reason The Kabbalah Centre often organizes spiritual pilgrimages to gravesites of the righteous. The best way to connect to the energy of Rabbi Akiva, for instance, is to visit his gravesite. However, since we know that the spiritual dimension contains neither time nor space, we can also access this Light for which he is still a special conduit by simply reading about or studying his work.

The Blessings of Humiliation

Most people might prefer physical torture to public embarrassment, not to mention humiliation. But according to Kabbalah, humiliation can be a sign that you're making headway against the ego and that the technology of Kabbalah is beginning to work its magic on your life. In fact, if you don't work to diminish your ego, there's no room for transformation.

This doesn't mean that you should attack someone else's ego (for their sake) or that someone can attack your ego without invitation. This is internal work, and by permission only. It's a painful process, but it paves the way to spiritual growth. Indeed, it's difficult to remain on the path of transformation if we're not fighting the ego.

The spiritual law that relates to our work on the ego is called Similarity of Form. Attracting the Light of the Creator requires a similarity on our part to the nature of the Creator; a nature that is sharing, giving, loving, inspiring, and creating. What separates us from the Light are those things that stand in opposition to It or that don't exist in It. Unlike us, the Light has no ego, nor any egotistic attributes, such as selfishness, insensitivity, jealousy, arrogance, or insecurity.

When we set the ego aside, we make room for the Light.

* * *

One day long ago, a student came across his teacher, the great kabbalist known as the Baal Shem Tov, standing outside a house of study. It was bitter cold outside, and through the window the student could see a warm fire along with a number of scholars talking with each other or reading from their spiritual texts.

Puzzled by the sight of his teacher standing out in the cold, the student said, "Master, why are you out here when you could be studying inside by the hearth?" The Baal Shem Tov looked at him and said, "There is no room for me in there." The student looked through the window again and said, "I don't understand. The house of study is half empty. There is plenty of room. Let's go in together."

The Baal Shem Tov smiled and replied, "There is no room for me here because the people inside are so full of themselves."

Kabbalah in a Public Forum

Those of you who have seen me speak in public might think I'm seeking out the kind of ego diminishment, or humiliation, we're talking about. You're not entirely wrong. I do speak in front of large audiences, sometimes thousands of people. And I know that I'm not one of those gifted motivational speakers you might see on TV. For one thing, I'm easily distracted. If a thought pops into my mind while I'm speaking, I can lose my train of thought right there, in front of everyone.

So why do I do it? Why do I put myself in a situation where people could very well ask themselves, "Why am I listening to this man who sometimes sounds as if he can barely put two thoughts together?" Well, for one thing, I believe passionately in my message and the energy it brings to people. I know that the technology of Kabbalah can awaken people and transform their lives. Sharing this wisdom is my calling; it's what I have to do.

The other reason is that I know that these moments when my limits as a public speaker become obvious are serving the goal of keeping my ego in check. This is especially important for people in my line of work; teachers are notoriously susceptible to developing oversized egos. So exposing myself to other people's judgment, and to some humiliation now and then, is a small price to pay for avoiding that dangerous trap. It's also a valuable reminder of the kabbalistic principle that it's the teachings that matter, not the teacher.

For many generations, great kabbalists have moved towards humiliation rather than away from it. When my parents started teaching Kabbalah, they knew that they would face derision and scorn. They knew that Kabbalah historically had been limited to the very few, and that some rabbis and scholars were going to be deeply threatened by their efforts now to make this wisdom, which we call a spiritual technology, available to everyone.

Did that stop them? No. They persevered, knowing that attempts to shame or humiliate them would only serve to hurt the ego. In this way, my parents faced the Opponent head on, and they still do so today. All great kabbalists have made this same choice, each in their own way.

A Story of Humiliation

Some 250 years ago, a kabbalist named Zusha broke with the tradition of staying in one village to build up a following of students. Instead, he chose to travel from town to town, teaching Kabbalah as the opportunity arose.

It so happened that as he was passing through one village, he noticed a large gathering of people, all of whom looked very unhappy. When he went over to find out what was going on, he was told that there had been a great wedding planned for the next day, but the bride's family had lost the dowry so the festivities had been cancelled.

Zusha asked, "Do you know how much money was lost?" They told him, and he went off. A few hours later, he returned and said, "I've found some money and I think it may be yours. It's in my room at the inn. But I need to know the exact denominations of the money you lost so I can be sure it belongs to you." The townspeople gave him the information, and off Zusha went.

A little later, he returned. "Yes, the denominations are correct. The money is yours." The crowd erupted in joy, slapping him happily on the back and thanking him. But Zusha quickly silenced them. "I've brought your money with me, and I hope you don't mind but I've deducted 30% as my finder's fee." In a flash, the joyful crowd turned ugly. The townspeople grabbed Zusha, took his purse full of money, beat him soundly, and chased him out of town.

By the time Zusha arrived home to his own village, the story of his greed has preceded him. The mayor was particularly incensed and demanded an explanation from Zusha's teacher. The teacher sent for Zusha, poured him a cup of tea, and calmly said, "I know what kind of man you are, so I also know there must be more to this story than what we've heard. Tell me your side of it, please." Clearly embarrassed, Zusha cleared his throat and began to speak.

He told his teacher and the mayor that for the past three months he had been saving and borrowing from relatives to pay the dowry for his own daughter's upcoming wedding. When he came across the downcast townspeople during his travels, he decided to give them his daughter's dowry to replace the one they had lost. He had asked for the specific denominations to make sure the money he produced exactly matched what had been lost.

Then he added, "But as I walked to the town square with the bag of money in my hand, I heard this voice inside me say, 'Zusha, how many people in the world would do what you are about to do? You are a remarkably generous and good-hearted man.' I started to feel so good about myself that I knew this was the voice of the Opponent. So I came up with the idea of demanding a finder's fee, knowing that the villagers would take the money, humiliate me, and run me out of town. In this way, I was able to do the right thing without succumbing to feeling self-important."

Seeking humiliation is one of the most effective ways to target the ego. We, ourselves, are not usually harmed by humiliation, but we've successfully scoured the ego, scrubbing away its ability to create an unduly elevated impression of ourselves. When we feel too good about ourselves, this represents only the 1% fulfillment. But by removing the ego, we make room for the 99% dimension to enter our lives and guide us. There is a reason why humiliation and humility are so similar: They are both vessels that contain Light.

Technology Beyond What's Normal

At The Kabbalah Centre, we talk a lot about achieving critical mass in the world— creating enough Light so we can start a chain reaction. One way to do this is to not just accept our negativity, but to expose it for all to see. Once again, Kabbalah turns prevailing wisdom on its head. Generally, we all try hard to hide our weaknesses but Kabbalah asks us to go public with them instead.

Another way to reduce the power of the ego is to do things that make absolutely no sense to the rational mind, like staying up all night or immersing ourselves in water (both acts being kabbalistic tools for transformation). Water has the spiritual quality of sharing. Find a swimming pool, lake, stream, or nearby beach and immerse yourself in it. We call this a *mikveh*. Then, while you're in the water, meditate on washing away your old, negative patterns of behavior. Let the water take them away, leaving you reborn as the leading actor/actress in a new movie of your own choosing. This experience can be like returning to the womb, like floating effortlessly on a sea of mother's love. This is the consciousness you can access through this practice. It may sound a bit strange, but it's a centuries-old technology that really works.

By doing things that take us outside of ordinary thinking, we can access previously untapped parts of our awareness.

Every new discovery is the result of challenging the status quo. If scientists were content with what they knew, society would never have enjoyed any scientific breakthroughs. Benjamin Franklin would never have contributed to our knowledge of electricity and Thomas Edison to our ability to communicate beyond the range of our voices.

If you and I give in to the naysayers, we'll never try anything new. If you traveled back in time just 30 years and talked about the cell phone or the Internet, no one would believe you. The lesson of history, over and over, is that things that make no sense, things that are considered impossible, can and do happen. With regularity.

I read the *Zohar* every day. I also like having it nearby in my house because I know the *Zohar* offers me and my family protection, just as it has done for kabbalists for a thousand years. I feel the same way about the Red String. Does it actually make sense that a string on my wrist can protect me from negative energy? Does it make sense that water can contain positive energy? Not really, but I know both to be true.

Déjà vu doesn't make sense either, but it's not uncommon. Does love make sense? Is it logical? Is it possible that those things that don't make sense may be more real than the things that do? The Rav likes to call what we do with Kabbalah "26th century physics." It may sound crazy, but when you get crazy in the world of technology, you get miracles.

So think of what you're reading as 26th century physics. One day, scientists will understand how all of this kabbalistic technology operates. In the meantime, why not take advantage of it, even if you don't yet understand the mechanisms involved? You don't know how the microwave works but you still use it to heat your food. You may not understand the technology of the Red String or the *Zohar* but why not try something when people consistently report that it works?

I'm not suggesting that you commit to anything based on blind faith. Try it out first. Try seeking humiliation. Give it some time, and if it doesn't do anything for you, then stop. But don't set it aside just because it doesn't make sense. Challenge the conventions of script writing. Challenge the old plot and you can create the lasting changes you're looking for.

If enough of us lived our lives this way, perhaps we could create a quantum shift to a world in which we would all make decisions based on the welfare of others. Imagine what living in a world like that would be like!

Rewriting Your Script

For our exercise in this chapter, seek out places in your life where you can do things that don't make any sense. Give this some thought, and then make a list. Take a look at this list from time to time. Do those things in your life that don't make sense seem to be delivering some surprising benefits?

Chapter 11

The Teaching Power of Pain

All of us fall down sometimes, whether it's in our relationships, our professional life or spiritual work. But when we want nothing more than to just give up, this is the time to persevere. When we feel most compelled to run, this is the time to stay. Because this is the time we can reveal the most Light.

If you're in a love relationship, I'm not saying that you necessarily have to stay in it long-term, but if you run away from a particular issue that suddenly comes up with your partner, you may be missing a golden opportunity to push through that obstacle and transform. We've seen that as we grow and evolve, the world around us improves, too.

The primary force that compels us to run or to give up is pain; the job, the marriage, the low self-esteem, the money struggle. We can't take it so we find ways to numb ourselves, including the addictions we explored in Chapter 9.

If you want to know where to find the Light inside you, it's just beyond the pain. Whenever pain shows up, work through it to get to the gold on the other side. In the same way that addiction points to our baggage, pain points to our Light. Avoidance may seem like a good strategy, but it keeps us from uncovering our purpose. People who are consistently successful are usually good at taking on pain rather than avoiding it. Athletes are a great case in point: They're poster children for the benefits of embracing hardship and fighting through pain.

A few years ago, my father suffered a stroke and my whole world went dark. There are still nights when I can't sleep for sadness, times when I think about the conversations I want to have with him, the things I'd like us to do together. (My father's recovery has been remarkable but things are not the way they once were.) Once I had made it through the worst of the pain, it became clear to me what I needed to do with my life, and I've become much more productive.

Instead of letting that pain keep me stuck in the past, I'm discovering my purpose. I'm doing my work and some of my father's as well. Hopefully, his vision of giving Kabbalah to the whole world will continue to unfold through me.

Helping Someone Else through Pain

When we go through a traumatic experience, that pain often gets trapped inside us. One powerful way we can resolve that trauma is by helping somebody else get through their own version of it.

Have you ever heard the phrase "the wounded healer"? Wounded healers have, themselves, experienced the very injury or illness they are now devoted to healing. They are unusually effective, which makes perfect sense. I'd feel better getting help from someone who knows exactly what I'm going through, and I'm sure you would, too.

By lifting up others who've been through the same troubles we have, we make a powerful connection to the Light. When we share our challenges with someone who's working through the same issues, we find release and so do they. And as always, the greater the challenge, the greater the Light that will be revealed. Most of us bury the really painful stuff as deeply as we can. The problem is that we're burying potential Light at the same time. We bring that Light to the surface by sharing that pain with someone else.

Kabbalah doesn't promise us that we're going to get to a place where life is a bed of roses. We all have chaos in our lives but the chaos doesn't have to stop us. In fact, it's actually meant to help us become who we need to be. It took me many months to come to terms with my father's stroke. More than once I thought, *I can't handle this.* But I forced myself to get through it by telling myself, I'm going to do this so that I can serve my family, my students, and the world.

External and Internal Light

The beauty of Kabbalah is that even though we can't change history, we can change the energy that history generates. When we go back into our past and relive what took place with a new consciousness, we alter the seed of that event and thereby change the tree that grows from it. We can't change what happened but by changing how we think, feel, and act around what happened, we can alter how it affects us.

My father used to say that pain is a teacher but it doesn't have to be our only teacher. When you were a child, you may have touched a hot pot or pan and burned yourself. If you're like me, you probably did that a few times, but eventually you learned to be careful handling pots and pans that had just come off the stove.

But is this the only way we learn to avoid pain—to experience it over and over again until we get the message forcefully enough?

In our physical dimension, the Light of the Creator takes two forms: *Inner or Internal Light* and *Surrounding Light*. We're born with a huge infusion of Light that travels with us through this life, accompanying our soul on its journey. Most of this is Surrounding Light, very little of it Inner Light. However, that Surrounding Light becomes internalized when we work through our pain, when we break through our patterns, when we stop seeking approval, when we share selflessly.

Just as there are two kinds of Light, there are two ways to change in this world. One is from the inside, when we awaken our consciousness and wrest control away from the ego. The other is from the outside, by paying attention to the knocking on our door that comes from the difficulties we're facing that don't seem to get any easier.

One way or another, we're going to transform, whether in this lifetime or in the ones that follow. But do we have to wait until those external forces bang our door down before we're motivated to change? Or can we choose a shorter route?

The universe doesn't put pressure on us all at once. At first, it taps us gently on the shoulder: Maybe with a job that isn't going well or some minor surgery that is needed. If we don't pay attention, though, we get a more forceful tap: Say, perhaps a fender-bender accident on the highway. If that doesn't wake us up, the universe raises the ante: Possibly with a good friend dying of cancer. Still nothing? Now we have to undergo major surgery.

The point is that the Surrounding Light needs to come in. Until major chaos upends us, most of us don't get serious about taking responsibility for our lives. But our Surrounding Light is going to keep up the pressure until we start turning it into Inner Light.

According to the laws of physics, the surrounding pressure of the water should crush a submarine in the depths of the ocean. To keep this from happening, much of a sub's energy is used to create an equal and opposite force through its pressurized hull. This is a great way to understand the relationship between Surrounding Light and Inner Light. Although the Surrounding Light's pressure on us isn't intended to be crushing, it does want us to push back, to elevate spiritually in ways that transform it to Inner Light. When we do so, we're going to see positive changes.

We all have pressures in life. We also have stress. Kabbalistically, pressure is a good thing but stress is not. Pressure motivates us to move forward; stress can make life unbearable. But it turns out the two forces are related. First comes pressure. Do we raise our own internal pressure to match it? Do we grow and become more from it? Do we respond to it by becoming a more conscious human being? If we don't, that pressure becomes stress. It's entirely up to us whether we let the pressure of the universe become stress or use that pressure to move us to greater consciousness.

The Power of Aramaic

Kabbalists find great power in Aramaic letters and believe that there are sacred sequences of these letters that can give us access to the endless energy of the Light. This power isn't just available to the tiny community of scholars that can actually read Aramaic. It works like music. You don't have to be able to read music to be touched by its beauty; you just have to listen to it. With Aramaic letters, you just have to look at them to access their power. And like musical notes, different sequences of Aramaic letters lead to varied expressions of their energy.

Have you ever had the experience of seeing a stranger across the room and feeling as if you already know that person? This intense communication is taking place just through eye contact. I'm sure you've heard the expression "the eyes are windows to the soul." This is something kabbalists have known for a very long time. Aramaic letters work on the principle that every time you make visual contact with one of the sacred sequences, you're tuning in to a spiritual frequency in the universe; think of it as a musical chime vibrating in your soul.

All this leads us to the Prayer of the Kabbalist, called the *Ana Beko'ach* in Aramaic. This prayer, derived from the *Book of Genesis*, has 42 sequences. Kabbalists believe that the letters of the first five books of the Bible can grant us special access to the energies of the universe. The Aramaic letters of Genesis provide a vessel for connecting to the seeds of Creation, to the beginning of everything. What better place to turn for transformation than Genesis, where it all began?

On page 93, you'll see the *Ana Beko'ach*, the Prayer of the Kabbalist, in its original Aramaic letters along with an English transliteration. For this exercise, I'd like you to scan the letters and say the words out loud, one by one.

These 42 ancient sequences are designed to help us move from wherever we are now to a new space where we can better connect to the Light. These letters act as a spiritual elevator that takes us up above this physical dimension of matter, raising our consciousness so we can see the bigger picture and pull ourselves out of our current mess.

Be sure to scan the letters from right to left, which is how Aramaic was written and read. You'll notice that there is an eighth line in smaller type, which you scan visually, but unlike the other lines, you don't actually say this line out loud.

I'd like to encourage you to read and say this kabbalistic prayer daily. It's a great tool for protection and for heightening consciousness.

❶ חסד, יום ראשון Sunday, Chesed

אבג יתץ

אָנָּא בְּכֹחַ. גְּדוּלַת יְמִינֶךָ. תַּתִּיר צְרוּרָה:

ana beko'ach gedulat yeminecha tatir tzerura

❷ גבורה, יום שני Monday, Gevurah

קרע שטן

קַבֵּל רִנַּת. עַמְּךָ שַׂגְּבֵנוּ. טַהֲרֵנוּ נוֹרָא:

kabel rinat amecha sagvenu taharenu nora

❸ תפארת, יום שלישי Tuesday, Tiferet

נגד יכש

נָא גִבּוֹר. דּוֹרְשֵׁי יִחוּדְךָ. כְּבָבַת שָׁמְרֵם:

na gibor dorshei yichudecha kevavat shomrem

❹ נצח, יום רביעי Wednesday, Netzach

בטר צתג

בָּרְכֵם טַהֲרֵם. רַחֲמֵי צִדְקָתֶךָ. תָּמִיד גָּמְלֵם:

barchem taharem rachamei tzidkatecha tamid gomlem

❺ הוד, יום חמישי Thursday, Hod

חקב טנע

חֲסִין קָדוֹשׁ. בְּרוֹב טוּבְךָ. נַהֵל עֲדָתֶךָ:

chasin kadosh berov tuvcha nahel adatecha

❻ יסוד, יום שישי Friday, Yesod

יגל פזק

יָחִיד גֵּאֶה. לְעַמְּךָ פְּנֵה. זוֹכְרֵי קְדוּשָׁתֶךָ:

yachid ge'eh le'amcha penei zochrei kedushatecha

❼ מלכות, שבת Saturday, Malchut

שקו צית

שַׁוְעָתֵנוּ קַבֵּל. וּשְׁמַע צַעֲקָתֵנוּ. יוֹדֵעַ תַּעֲלוּמוֹת:

shav'atenu kabel ushma tza'akatenu yode'a ta'alumot

(בלחש) בָּרוּךְ שֵׁם כְּבוֹד מַלְכוּתוֹ, לְעוֹלָם וָעֶד:

(silently) baruch shem kevod malchuto le'olam va'ed

Scanning Direction

93

Chapter 12

Fellowship in the Light

You can only go so far by yourself in this process of transformation because it's so difficult to see your own ego at work. Moreover, from a spiritual perspective, we are all one. When we do our spiritual work together with a friend, we can be strong where perhaps the friend is not so strong, and our friend can be compassionate where we are not. In this way, we can function as one complete person rather than two incomplete parts.

My father's favorite story describes the kind of unity that can be attained through friendship, while at the same time revealing the secret for averting a decree of judgment heading our way. As you'll see, the Creator would never allow judgment to befall someone who doesn't deserve it, even if this means that someone who does deserve it will have that judgment removed.

A Tale of Two Friends

Once there were two friends, one of whom was arrested for a theft he had committed years earlier as a street urchin. He was brought before the king, who sentenced him to die. When the man begged the king to give him three days to put his affairs in order, the king replied, "How do I know you're going to come back?"

The sentenced man said, "My best friend will stay in prison until I return. I would never let him die, especially not for something I have done." The king accepted this temporary exchange as bond, but he cautioned the felon that if he was even a minute late, his friend would die.

So the condemned man went off to put his affairs in order. But at the end of the three days, there was no sign of him. The king said, "Prepare the thief's friend for execution."

Just as the executioner finished sharpening his blade, the crowd parted for a man who galloped up on a lathered horse, calling, "Wait, wait, I'm here to receive my punishment. Don't execute that man." Bowing low before the king, the sentenced man explained, "Your Highness, I was delayed by highwaymen who attacked me on the road. But I here I am. If justice is to be served, please free my friend and let me die in his place."

But his friend, who was still kneeling before the grim-faced executioner, shouted, "No, Your Highness. He was late; therefore you must live up to your promise and execute me instead. I refuse to live without my friend."

The king watched in amazement as each man argued his case for why he should die and his friend should go free.

Finally the king turned to the convicted thief and said, "When I sentenced you to death, I was punishing one person for the crime you committed. But now I see that if I proceed according to my word, I must punish two. This I will not do." So the king set both men free.

And he was so impressed by the depth of their friendship that he invited them to join his court and showered them with honors.

Rewriting Your Script

Consider your friends and identify someone who could be your spiritual partner, a person you could trust fully. Tell this friend what you're experiencing, and be open to what he or she going through. We all need companions on our journey. We can only go so far on our own.

Chapter 13

Kabbalistic Astrology

Kabbalists believe that a knowledge of astrology can help us successfully navigate the chaos in our lives. At the time of your birth, the stars were in a specific alignment that makes you prone to certain patterns of behavior. Not only does knowing this help you understand yourself, but it can guide you to interact more successfully with others.

It's important to remember that astrology deals in patterns, not destiny. As my father always says, "forces impel, but they don't compel." Your astrological chart is a valuable tool for identifying your strengths as well as the tendencies you need to overcome.

When we look for organizing principles in the twelve astrological signs, we find four groups of elements, with three signs under each element. The four elements are:

Air (Gemini, Libra, and Aquarius)
Water (Cancer, Scorpio, and Pisces)
Fire (Aries, Leo, and Sagittarius)
Earth (Taurus, Virgo, and Capricorn)

Before we consider each sign, I'd like to suggest that you don't just to focus on your own sign. We all need to know about every one of these 12 signs. Your parents, kids, partners, bosses, business colleagues, and friends all have positive and negative tendencies based on their signs. They all have hot buttons and specific work to do in this lifetime. The more we know about the people around us, the better we can make our lives together. The more we know about astrological signs, the more skillfully we can navigate the world.

There are entire books written on this topic, but for our purposes here, I'll briefly go through each sign to give you a sense of kabbalistic astrology, and we'll see how it helps us in our corrective process. I'll be mentioning the proactive, or positive, side of each sign, as well as its reactive, or difficult, aspect.

Air Signs: Gemini, Libra, and Aquarius

I'm a Gemini, so let's begin with the air signs. Air signs tend to be analytical, intellectual, and cerebral. The positive aspect of Gemini is communicative, intellectual, and curious. The reactive aspect is a tendency to be indecisive. Knowing this, I strive to focus on detail as well as seeing the big picture, on finishing what I start, and on putting my trust in the Light.

The next air sign is Libra. The proactive aspect of Libra is the desire for harmony: Libras tend to be friendly and loving. The reactive side of this sign is Libras tendency to avoid confrontation and conflict, and to want to be a people-pleaser. Libras commitment to change might require developing the ability to make decisions without fear of what others may think and then to stick to them. Not questioning past decisions and sharing for the right reasons, this is the task for Libras.

My Aquarius friends tend to be on the wild side, a bit out there. Their proactive tendency is to be humanitarian, free spirits with a desire to change the world for the better. On the reactive side, Aquarians have a difficult time with structure and control. Aquarians need to fight the urge to always be unique and try being team players instead. If you're an Aquarius, practice compassion. Make dependability a habit. Transform ego into humility. Build relationships.

Generally speaking, if you want to communicate effectively with an air sign, you have to connect to their mind, because if you seek the heart first, you may not find anybody home. Once you've reached an air sign intellectually, they'll open their heart. Trying it the other way around does not work nearly as well.

Water Signs: Cancer, Scorpio, and Pisces

Cancer's proactive nature is emotional, sensitive, and nurturing. Cancers make great parents and wonderful cooks. On the reactive side, they're moody and they tend to grapple frequently with depression. Cancers need to commit to letting go of things that promise security. They need to let go of their fears. They need to be less possessive, take more risks, trust the Light more, engage in frequent acts of sharing, and count their blessings every day. Most importantly, Cancers need to live in the present and avoid brooding over events from the past.

Scorpios are very intense. Proactive by nature, they're loyal and passionate, and they have a tremendous amount of drive. Their reactive side comes out when that energy gets extreme, when it can also manifest in the form of anger and vengefulness. A reactive Scorpio can be self-destructive. Scorpios need to commit to self-love, to avoid judging or being jealous of others, to staying calm, and to avoid falling into crisis mode. Scorpios need to achieve fulfillment through self-control, not by controlling others. Most importantly, Scorpios need to make a commitment to being happy and to inviting in the Light.

The proactive nature of a classic Pisces is to be sensitive, spiritual, and grounded. Their reactive side is that they're constantly looking to be comfortable, which moves them in the direction of escapism and addiction. Pisceans tend to be highly influenced by their environment. Pisceans should commit to being leaders not followers, to taking the initiative, to balancing logic and emotion, to handling pressure with certainty, to going the extra mile, and to feeling other people's pain, not just their own. Kabbalistically, Pisceans tend to be old souls.

Fire Signs: Aries, Leo, and Sagittarius

The next signs we're going to tackle are the fire signs. Fire signs have tremendous power. The question is: What will they do with it?

The proactive side of Aries is a big desire, which is considered a great asset kabbalistically. Aries wants to grow, which is wonderful, given that this is our fundamental mission in life. On the reactive side, Aries tend to focus on themselves, often to the exclusion of others. Aries also tend not to finish what they start and have difficulty listening to others. Aries need to commit to completing things and to remembering the past to avoid making the same mistakes next time. Aries need to ask the Light for guidance in remembering that we are all simply channels for the Light; they must also learn to empathize with others and try to avoid conflict. Aries need to find peace within themselves as a way to minimize conflict with other people.

Leos can be tough, but they're also exciting and creative. Their proactive nature is very loving and generous. Their reactive side is overly protective, with a tendency to be dominant and egotistical. Leos also tend to be a little lazy. They need to commit to letting go of their desire to control and trying to be everyone's friend. They need to think before they speak and to use their strength to help others, not dominate them. Leos benefit from being more compassionate, from understanding the perspective of others, from being sensitive to other people's feelings, and from not always trying to be the center of attention.

The proactive side of Sagittarius is the tendency to be optimistic, learned, and philosophical. Their reactive aspect is that they can have a heart of stone. Not only does information tend to be processed through their brain, but they don't express what they feel. Sagittarians can also be direct to the point of being tactless. Sagittarians need to stand for something they believe in, to not be complacent, to practice forgiveness, to pay attention to detail, to analyze the full situation before making a decision, to be more sensitive to others, and to watch what they say.

The most important thing about working with a fire sign is to be honest and to let them know when they're infringing on your territory. It's easy to enable a fire sign. Fire spreads quickly enough on its own, and most people add gasoline to the fire by being compliant. Our job is to make sure fire signs don't encroach on our space. By giving us space, they let us into their life.

Earth Signs: Virgo, Taurus, and Capricorn

Earth signs are our last element to cover. They tend to be practical, logical, and scientific. Each sign is different, of course, but earth signs share an emphasis on logic.

People born under the sign of Virgo pay amazing attention to detail. They're very organized and bottom-line oriented. They see right through distractions. If you want to know what's wrong in a given situation, ask a Virgo. They'll find it. The reactive aspect of this sign is critical, controlling, and perfectionist; everything has to be just right, and if it isn't, it can seem like the end of the world to a Virgo. The Virgo needs to commit to letting go of the desire to control, to asking questions, and to seeking to understand and not just judge. Virgos need to look for the good in everything and everyone.

The proactive aspect of Taurus includes good business sense and stability. Taurus's reactive tendency is to be possessive, to seek comfort, and to be stubborn. A Taurus will go to the same restaurant and order the same thing day after day after day. A Taurus needs to commit to embracing discomfort, listening to and actively sharing with others, and transforming complacency into action. Unfortunately, a Taurus can stay in a bad situation for a long time due to inertia, becoming comfortable with their chaos. Most importantly, it's not easy for a Taurus to transform spiritually, so if you're a Taurus, just keep on pushing.

The proactive nature of Capricorn is to be practical, responsible, and grounded. The Capricorn's reactive side is very materialistic and is controlled by fear. Fear of what they won't have is a powerful motivator for Capricorns. Capricorns need to trust that things will turn out okay (especially when they're not easy to achieve). Capricorns need to break some of their own rules, to take risks, to express emotion, and to understand that not everything has a purpose. Capricorns need to rely more on the 99% and less on the physical realm. Not everything has to be part of the plan; some things can just be. Capricorns start life very seriously, and as they get older, they start becoming sillier, which is the opposite of how most of us do it. This is a good development for Capricorns, who can benefit from taking life a little less seriously.

Now that we've looked at the 12 astrological signs, we can see more readily where our obstacles and opportunities lie. We can also see our fellow travelers more clearly. By observing their garbage as well as our own, we can advance our mutual mission of spiritual growth.

Rewriting Your Script

Below you'll see two columns. In the column on the left, list the reactive characteristics of your sign that have affected you. In the right-hand column, write down what you're going to do to address those characteristics and patterns.

Reactive	**Proactive**
Reactive characteristics of your sign that have affected you.	What are you going to do to balance these qualities?

Chapter 14

In Conclusion

I'd like to end this book with a story, so I offer you this one as a parting gift. Life consists of cycles—daily, weekly, monthly, annual, seasonal, and even personal—as we soar and tumble with each new joy and setback. I realize you have plenty of examples of this in your own life, but sometimes it's easier to see the hamster wheel we're on when we look outside ourselves.

The Man Who Lost All His Money

Once there were two men who went into business together. They prospered and eventually amassed a small fortune. Being ambitious, they decided to invest everything they'd made in a bigger venture with far wealthier merchants. One of the partners put their collective gold in a leather satchel and set out on a day's journey to join the other partner in a meeting with the merchants.

Weary of walking on the road, the man with the satchel lay down beneath a shady tree to rest. He made a pillow of his coat and fell asleep, but when he awoke, the satchel full of money was gone. He ran back out to the road to see if he could catch the thief, but there was no one around. He started to run frantically this way and that until, exhausted, he finally returned to the shady tree, fell to the ground, and began to weep. When he lifted his head, however, he saw the satchel of gold; it had been hidden by his coat.

When he rejoined his partner, he could barely tell the story; his near-brush with disaster had shaken him to the core. He told his partner, "I can't do this. I just can't live with nearly having lost everything we've both worked so hard to achieve. Go ahead and take your share of the money and invest it, but leave me out of it. From this day forward, we are no longer partners." His friend and business partner protested strenuously but to no avail, and they finally agreed to go their separate ways.

Time passed, and the man who believed he had lost their money saw his fortunes take an ill turn. His business dealings started to sour, and where once he had had a golden touch, now his every investment turned to ashes. He lost his wealth, his home, even his family.

One day, he was wandering and came upon a lake. Filthy, he shed his clothes, walked into the water, and set out to clean himself. When he returned to the shore, however, he found that his clothes were gone. Covering his nakedness with a large leaf, he began to laugh and dance joyfully.

A man in a nearby house heard him and came outside to see what was going on. As he warily approached the disheveled, joyful man, it struck him that there something about the fellow that seemed familiar. As he came a little closer, he realized, *Oh my, this is my former partner.* Inviting his old friend into his home, he listened to the story of his former partner's journey during their years apart. But when the story came to the moment that his old associate had lost everything, even his clothes, he asked, "So why are you so happy now? Have you lost your mind?"

His almost-naked friend replied, "When I was walking down the road with our sack of gold and I almost lost it all, I realized I was then at the top of the spinning wheel of life. I knew the only way for me to go from there was down, and I did not want to take you with me. Now that I have lost everything, even my last piece of clothing, I know that I have hit the very bottom and from here I can only go up."

The kabbalist who told this story ended it by saying, "Our job in life is to get off the wheel."

Ultimately, the only way we can achieve freedom from the cycles of pain and joy that are part of the 1% World is to reach a level of consciousness where we can draw more and more Light from the spiritual 99% Realm.

This is my deepest wish for you.

Appendix

Visiting Your Inner Movie Theater: Three Additional Exercises

A Visit to Your Inner Movie Theater: Cleaning the Garbage

So many of us carry pain from traumatic moments—pain that needs to be dredged up and set in front of us to be cleansed by the Light. That's what we're going to do right now with the following exercise. I'd like you to get comfortable in a place where you can sit uninterrupted for the next five minutes. Try not to cross your arms or legs or lean against anything, if possible.

Once you're comfortable, start to focus on your breathing. Every time you inhale, imagine yourself drawing in the Lightforce of the Creator; every time you exhale, imagine you're letting go of all the stress, anxiety, and difficult stuff you deal with every day. Breathe in and out like this several times. Relax your body, breathing into your tight places, starting with the top of your head and working your way down to your toes. Let the stress melt away.

Now I'd like you to create an internal personal safe place for yourself. Everyone's place is different. You're going to that place where you feel most relaxed, safe, and secure. Nothing can harm or touch you here. It might be a real place from your past, or it might be a place in your imagination. That doesn't matter. What does matter is that you fully experience your special place by engaging all your senses, allowing them to ground you in this safe place. If you're sitting on a beach, notice the colors of the sky, the water, and the sand. Listen to the cry of the seagulls, the waves crashing against the shore. Smell the salty tang in the air. Get in touch with the feeling of your body on the blanket or sand dune you're sitting on.

Now that you're established in this safe place, imagine that a doorway has suddenly materialized in the air before you. As you calmly get up and walk over to it, you see a set of stairs descending from the door. Curious, you step through the door and walk down the stairs, where you find yourself in a little home movie theater. Sit down in one of the big, plush seats facing a nice, wide screen.

As the lights slowly dim, a movie starts playing. It's a film in which you star; it's the story of all your traumatic life events, including the things you're most ashamed of. You're not alone in having had these experiences, but this is your movie. As the movie runs, you're simply watching it; you're not devoid of feeling by any means, but you're not upset. You're an objective observer.

You remind yourself that you're safe here, that it's just a movie. You're not judging, nor are you being judged. It's almost as if the star were someone else, whose most difficult life events you can view with compassion. Without being overwhelmed by these events, let yourself feel the pain, the loss, the regret, the sadness, the remorse. Go ahead, feel it; don't be afraid to pick up the garbage. It's going to make you stronger. It's going to help you transform.

Now visualize yourself holding this garbage up to the Light, which effortlessly and painlessly burns it up. The Light that's surrounding and protecting you incinerates every one of those feelings of remorse, anxiety, tension, stress, and pain. Those events happened in the past. We can't make the past disappear but by embracing all that pain and exposing it, you're allowing the Light to take care of it for you.

Now it's time to walk back up those steps to your special safe place. When you get there, reactivate your senses to ground yourself in the moment. This time, you're bringing a new awareness of the Light with you. It's still enveloping you, feeding you with energy, and protecting you.

This isn't an easy exercise, but each time you do it, you lighten your burden of past pain. It gets easier, which is why I encourage you to do it over and over again.

A Visit to Your Inner Movie Theater: Parent Work

The following exercise can be applied to any issue you may be working through. In this first example, I've focused on your relationship with your parents, but as you'll see in the two examples that follow, the format of this exercise can be tailored to fit any obstacle.

Make yourself comfortable. Find yourself a chair or another comfortable place to sit. Try to maintain an upright posture if you can, supporting yourself with your back straight and without crossing your arms or legs.

Every time you take in a breath, visualize yourself drawing in Light, drawing in the energy of Creation. When you breathe out, imagine yourself expelling all your anxiety, stress, and tension. Inhale Light; exhale chaos. As you do this, let your body relax. Let your facial muscles go slack, your neck loosen, your shoulders slump. Feel all your muscles become rubbery as a wave of relaxation moves slowly down your body until it reaches your toes. Breathe into the tight places in your body as you continue to relax.

Now go to your safe place and engage all your senses. Really ground yourself in this space where nothing can harm you, where you're surrounded by Light. Once again, imagine a doorway opening up in front of you, and see the stairs leading down to your private movie theater. Walk down and find yourself a comfortable seat in front of the nice, wide screen.

As you settle in, a movie begins to play on the screen before you. It's a documentary film, and its subject is your life—specifically how your parents treated you. At this moment, the emphasis is on the things your parents did that weren't fair, that may have felt abusive or painful. Just sit back and let the movie unfold, but don't engage in it the way you did in your special place. Just watch the movie with curiosity, allowing your feelings to arise and move on, like clouds scudding by on a windy day. Be cool. Relax. It's just a movie.

As you watch the images flickering on the screen, as you observe all the things you blame your parents for, start thanking your parents for their every action, especially the negative ones. Remember that your soul, not your ego, chose these specific parents so that it could advance and elevate itself. It chose your parents for what it could learn from them.

So if, for example, your parents weren't there for you as a child, if you felt abandoned, alone, or neglected, thank them for it. Those experiences were painful at the time (and may still be painful today), but they helped you realize that you are responsible for your life and what you do with it. Maybe you turned to the Light, or spirituality, because your parents weren't there for you.

Look at the behaviors you blame your parents for, then turn these behaviors around and consider how they're serving you, how they have helped and continue to help you develop the positive aspects of the person you are today. When you do this, you're beginning to look at your parents and your life through the eyes of your soul. This is the consciousness that leads to spiritual growth and transformation.

Remember not to let yourself get caught up in your emotional reactions to the movie. You're simply watching, allowing your feelings to come and go before saying to your parents, "Thank you for letting me be independent; it taught me to be resourceful. Thank you for being demanding; it taught me how bring out the best in myself."

In cases of serious abuse, it's helpful to know that you're not alone, and that sometimes we're working out our *tikkun* for reasons we can't see right now. But rest assured that everything that's happened is all part of a spiritual process, part of a bigger system devoted to expanding your soul. The more you embrace what happened to you, the quicker the process will be.

You may have heard the expression: "You can't let go of something until you're holding it." It's true. So embrace your experiences as a child with your parents. Then let those experiences go, thanking your parents for giving your soul what it needed.

After you've rewound this portion of your movie and reviewed it a few times, let the lights go back on in the movie theater. Walk out and back up the stairs to your safe place. Now re-engage your senses. What do you see? What do you smell? What are the sounds around you? Can you taste something in the air? As you consider the message of the movie, remember that all those events of your past were part of a higher purpose. The Opponent controls your body, but your soul needed to go through what it did so that you could become a more elevated human being.

You could still choose to be selfish. The choice is always yours, but make sure to choose wisely. The problem with being selfish or with playing the victim is that you pay for it with frustration, loneliness, and long-term unhappiness. Kabbalah gives us the awareness that we can choose to do something different with our experiences, that we can choose to grow, to be better, to open our hearts.

I want you to fully experience that choice—the choice of gratitude for those things that made you a better person—and lock it in. Make it part of you. Make it part of your safe, special place. Anchor it. Now take a deep breath, and then let your breath out slowly and completely. Know that you always have the ability to transform any past event into a soul lesson that will help you soar higher than you ever dreamed possible.

Welcome to the eyes of the soul.

A Visit to Your Inner Movie Theater: Eliminating Those Buttons

Find yourself a comfortable chair or couch to sit on. In kabbalistic meditation, we encourage people not to cross their arms or legs. Try to sit with your back straight so that you are not leaning against anything. You can leave your hands relaxed on your legs, palms facing each other.

Start to pay attention to your breathing. Take a few deep breaths, and as you inhale, breathe in the Lightforce of the Creator. As you exhale, let go of any tension, stress, or anxiety you may be feeling.

Keep breathing normally, and go to your safe place. Once you're there, use your various senses to engage with your surroundings, much as you did in the previous exercises. You're safe here. No one can harm you.

Once again, visualize the doorway opening to the steps leading down into your personal movie theater. As you find a comfortable chair in the theater, the lights dim and a movie starts playing in front of you. You're the subject of this movie, too, but this time you're being confronted by someone who really pushes your buttons. This person is controlling, or inconsiderate, or selfish, or mean, or arrogant— whatever it is that upsets you most. As you watch your reactions, think about the fact that this other person's behavior wouldn't affect you so much if it didn't resonate with you.

Make the shift from looking at the other person's reactive behavior and thinking, *That's terrible, I would never do that,* to the thought that maybe you do exactly that, albeit in your own way.

As before, take an inner step back from the strong feelings on the screen and watch them with curiosity. You're here to learn from this movie. Now imagine yourself going up to that person on the screen who upsets you so much. Look the person in the eye and extend your arms to hug him or her, saying, "Thank you for showing me how I can be intolerant, or manipulative, or insincere. Thank you for showing me where I need to do my work." In cases of abuse, you can say, "Thank you for showing me my Light and teaching me how to protect it."

The more we fight against the lessons the universe is trying to teach us, the longer it takes to reach the lasting fulfillment that awaits us. By identifying what comes up for you and by thanking that person for being your teacher, you're taking ownership. You're growing in your spiritual work.

Now imagine that the next time someone behaves rudely, or aggressively, or insincerely—either to you or to someone else—you can observe it without getting upset. It's just behavior, after all. It's happening, which isn't fun, but you don't have to get fired up about it. Now your reaction is no longer in charge. You are.

The movie screen has gone blank and the lights have come up in the theater, so you walk back up the steps and out to your safe place. Now re-engage in your surroundings with your senses. They're the same, and yet everything has changed. When your hot-button issues come up now, you're not going to get upset. You feel lighter, more relaxed and alert. You've identified the Opponent within you and you've said to him, "You can't control me anymore because I know your name."

Take a few deep breaths, open your eyes, and welcome this newly arrived version of yourself.

More Ways to Bring the Wisdom of Kabbalah into Your Life

The Power of Kabbalah
By Yehuda Berg

The familiar reality is the physical 1 percent material realm in which we live, yet there is another dimension—the world beyond our five senses. According to Kabbalah, this is called the 99 percent realm. Everything we truly desire: love, joy, peace of mind, freedom, is available when we connect to the 99 percent reality. The problem is that most of us have inadvertently disconnected ourselves from this dimension. Imagine if we could access this source at will, and on a continuing basis. This is the power of Kabbalah. This foundational text features new content and is more accessible for meeting today's current challenges. Use the exercises included to break free of prevalent beliefs and habits which lead to negativity. Readers will discover how to align their actions with their higher purpose, and become conscious of the unlimited possibilities in their own life.

The Living Kabbalah System App
By Yehuda Berg

The Living Kabbalah System is an app for transforming your life. Brought to you by bestselling author and spiritual teacher Yehuda Berg, this powerful 23-day, step-by-step, system is complete with practical tools, audio sessions, and exercises. Track your progress, see results, and take your life to the next level. Now available for iPad and iPhone.

Consciousness and the Cosmos
By Rav Berg

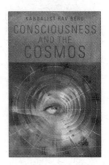

Within the pages of *Consciousness and the Cosmos*, Kabbalist Rav Beg investigates quantum physics, astrology and the Bible, and uncovers a link between them. He delves into subjects ranging from extraterrestrials, to parallel universes, and the Tree of Life. Throughout it all he posits that random chance is non-existent: Things that happen through a conjunction of events, whether moments apart or centuries removed, are intimately related.

Through the information presented, we come to understand that Time is the distance between Cause and Effect. If one can go back in time and change the cause (the seed) then one can change the effect (the tree). This book reveals how to use consciousness to travel through time and space, and how to tap the forces of intelligence that pervade our cosmos.

For readers who are interested in science and question the Bible, and for readers who cherish the Bible and question science, this book provides a logical bridge. Humanity is at the center; we affect everything that happens. Rav Berg unveils a kabbalistic view of the universe, which proposes that mankind is not only a participant but a determinator of all energy activity. Every event, every action, every idea is connected through the human mind by the network that is the cosmos. Humanity, through our consciousness, determines what occurs in the world.

Energy of the Hebrew Letters
By Rav Berg

The *Zohar* tells us that one of God's first creations was the twenty-two letters of the Hebrew alphabet. But these letters are far more than the simple symbols of communication that would later be used in a galley of type. Kabbalists teach that the Hebrew letters are like wires, a technology for transferring energy from the Light of God into the physical world. The allegory of the letters as they pleaded their respective cases for the primary role in God's creative process is the blueprint by which Creation was made possible.

Rav Berg illustrates the bedrock of Kabbalah, and poetically reveals the spiritual meaning and history of each of the twenty-two letters: How and why it was created, and what energy it transmits to us.

...To Be Continued...: Reincarnation & the Purpose of Our Lives
By Karen Berg

Reincarnation is the soul's journey back to the Light via multiple physical incarnations. In each lifetime, the soul returns to the physical world to correct a different aspect of itself. In one incarnation a soul may need to learn about being rich; another it may need to learn about being poor. Or it may need to experience strength and weakness, anger and compassion, beauty and unsightliness. Awareness of our soul's journey creates a context that helps us to guide our lives and appreciate what we were given. With this knowledge over many lifetimes our soul eventually manages to understand all the lessons and puts all of these fragments together. As it does so, the soul gathers sparks of Light back to itself. Eventually it returns to the source of all Light—the Creator—complete. When we understand reincarnation, our mistakes in this life don't become devastating. We develop a level of spiritual maturity that helps us to perceive how everything is part of a bigger plan designed to help us to change and grow. Death is not the end of the game, but just a chance to do over. We have nothing to fear. Life will be continued.

Becoming Like God
By Michael Berg

Becoming Like God offers a revolutionary method for becoming all powerful. Written with extraordinary clarity, Michael Berg presents a logical approach to achieving our supreme birthright. In revealing this opportunity for humanity, he highlights ways to develop our natural God-like attributes, and diminish the aspects of our nature that interfere with our destiny. In his succinct style, Michael provides the answer to the eternal question of why we are here: To become like God.

The *Zohar*

Composed more than 2,000 years ago, the 23-volume *Zohar* is a commentary on biblical and spiritual matters written in the form of conversations among teachers. It was given to all humankind by the Creator to bring us protection, to connect us with the Creator's Light, and ultimately to fulfill our birthright of transformation. The *Zohar* is an effective tool for achieving our purpose in life.

More than eighty years ago, when The Kabbalah Centre was founded, the *Zohar* had virtually disappeared from the world. Today, all this has changed. Through the editorial efforts of Michael Berg, the *Zohar* is available in the original Aramaic language and for the first time in English with commentary.

We teach Kabbalah, not as a scholarly study but as a way of creating a better life and a better world.

WHO WE ARE

The Kabbalah Centre is a non-profit organization that makes the principles of Kabbalah understandable and relevant to everyday life. The Kabbalah Centre teachers provide students with spiritual tools based on kabbalistic principles that students can then apply as they see fit to improve their own lives and by doing so, make the world better. The Centre was founded by Rav Yehuda Ashlag in 1922 and now spans the globe with brick-and-mortar locations in more than 40 cities as well as an extensive online presence. To learn more, visit www.kabbalah.com.

WHAT WE TEACH

There are five core principles:

- **Sharing:** Sharing is the purpose of life and the only way to truly receive fulfillment. When individuals share, they connect to the force of energy that Kabbalah calls the Light—the Infinite Source of Goodness, the Divine Force, the Creator. By sharing, one can overcome ego—the force of negativity.

- **Awareness and Balance of the Ego:** The ego is a voice inside that directs people to be selfish, narrow-minded, limited, addicted, hurtful, irresponsible, negative, angry, and hateful. The ego is a main source of problems because it allows us to believe that others are separate from us. It is the opposite of sharing and humility. The ego also has a positive side, as it motivates one to take action. It is up to each individual to choose whether they act for themselves or whether to also act in the well-being of others. It is important to be aware of one's ego and to balance the positives and negatives.

- **Existence of Spiritual Laws:** There are spiritual laws in the universe that affect people's lives. One of these is the Law of Cause and Effect: What one puts out is what one get back, or what we sow is what we reap.

- **We Are All One:** Every human being has within him- or herself a spark of the Creator that binds each and every person into one totality. This understanding informs us of the spiritual precept that every human being must be treated with dignity at all times, under any circumstances. Individually, everyone is responsible for war and poverty in all parts of the world and individuals can't enjoy true and lasting fulfillment as long as others are suffering.

- **Leaving Our Comfort Zone Can Create Miracles:** Becoming uncomfortable for the sake of helping others taps us into a spiritual dimension that ultimately brings Light and positivity to our lives.

HOW WE TEACH

Courses and Classes. On a daily basis, The Kabbalah Centre focuses on a variety of ways to help students learn the core kabbalistic principles. For example, The Centre develops courses, classes, online lectures, books, and audio products. Online courses and lectures are critical for students located around the world who want to study Kabbalah but don't have access to a Kabbalah Centre in their community.

Spiritual Services and Events. The Centre organizes and hosts a variety of weekly and monthly events and spiritual services where students can participate in lectures, meditation and share meals together. Some events are held through live streaming online. The Centre organizes spiritual retreats and tours to energy sites, which are places that have been closely touched by great kabbalists. For example, tours take place at locations where kabbalists may have studied or been buried, or where ancient texts like the *Zohar* were authored. International events provide students from all over the world with an opportunity to make connections to unique energy available at certain times of the year. At these events, students meet with other students, share experiences and build friendships.

Volunteering. In the spirit of Kabbalah's principles that emphasize sharing, The Centre provides a volunteer program so that students can participate in charitable initiatives, which includes sharing the wisdom of Kabbalah itself through a mentoring program. Every year, hundreds of student volunteers organize projects that benefit their communities such as feeding the homeless, cleaning beaches and visiting hospital patients.

One-on-One. The Kabbalah Centre seeks to ensure that each student is supported in his or her study. Teachers and mentors are part of the educational infrastructure that is available to students 24 hours a day, seven days a week.

Hundreds of teachers are available worldwide for students as well as a study program for their continued development. Study takes place in person, by phone, in study groups, through webinars, and even self-directed study in audio format or online.

Mentorship. The Centre's mentor program provides new students with a mentor to help them better understand the kabbalistic principles and teachings. The mentors are experienced Kabbalah students who are interested in supporting new students.

Publishing. Each year, The Centre translates and publishes some of the most challenging kabbalistic texts for advanced scholars including the *Zohar*, *Writings of the Ari*, and the *Ten Luminous Emanations with Commentary*. Drawing from these sources The Kabbalah Centre publishes books yearly in more than 30 languages that are tailored for both beginner- and intermediate-level students and distributed around the world.

Museum. The Centre gathers and preserves original kabbalistic texts and rare manuscripts that are housed in a Los Angeles museum. The texts are made available online for students and scholars to view.

***Zohar* Project.** The *Zohar*, the primary text of kabbalistic wisdom, is a commentary on biblical and spiritual matters composed and compiled over 2000 years ago and is believed to be a source of Light. Kabbalists believe that when it is brought into areas of darkness and turmoil, the *Zohar* can create change and bring about improvement. The Kabbalah Centre's *Zohar* Project shares the *Zohar* in 95 countries by distributing free copies to organizations and individuals in recognition of their service to the community and to areas where there is danger. In the past year, over 50,000 copies of the *Zohar* were donated to hospitals, embassies, places of worship, universities, not-for-profit organizations, emergency services, war zones, natural disaster locations, soldiers, pilots, government officials, medical professionals, humanitarian aid workers, and more.

Everything we have learned from The Centre has brought so much blessing to our lives that we are grateful to be able to dedicate Yehuda's book and the life changing wisdom that he shares with the world. May its publishing and distribution bring change and Light to the lives of those who read it.

This dedication is in appreciation for the Rav and Karen for risking everything and working so hard to open the doors so that everyone can learn these principles. Thank you to Yehuda and Michael Berg for continuing the work.

Karen, a special additional thank you for the Kabbalah Children's Academy, which has brought Light and happiness to our daughter's experience of school.

Thank you to our spiritual teachers, Moshe and Ruth Rosenberg, who guide us gently and firmly to change and grow every day as true soul mates.

And to all the Chevre and teachers of the world, especially Ariel, David and Tzipora.

Camilo, Vanessa & Andrea.